# the economics of
# MACRO
## issues
## second edition

**Roger LeRoy MILLER**
*Institute for University Studies*
*Arlington, Texas*

**Daniel K. BENJAMIN**
*Clemson University*
*and PERC, Bozeman, Montana*

Boston San Francisco New York
London Toronto Sydney Tokyo Singapore Madrid
Mexico City Munich Paris Cape Town Hong Kong Montreal

Editor-in-Chief: Denise Clinton
Acquisitions Editor: Roxanne Hoch
Editorial Assistant: Julia Boyles
Managing Editor: Jim Rigney
Sr. Production Supervisor: Katherine Watson
Design Manager: Gina Kolenda
Sr. Manufacturing Buyer: Hugh Crawford
Production House: Orr Book Services
Composition: Nesbitt Graphics, Inc.
Cover Image: © PictureQuest

ISBN: 0-321-30359-8

Library of Congress Control Number: 2004028912

1 2 3 4 5 6 7 8 9 10—DOC—09 08 07 06 05

# Dedication

To Jon Engen,

You continue to
inspire me to
do better, and for
that (and much more)
I thank you.

R.L.M


To the menory of Jim Diss,
and to Ray Nault and Dennis Semprini,

Whose intense work has made possible
great events for me and countless others.

D.K.B

# Contents

# Suggestions for Use

At the request of our readers, we include the following table to help you incorporate the chapters of this book into your syllabus. Depending on the breadth of your course, you may also want to consult the companion paperback, *The Economics of Public Issues, 14th Edition*, which features microeconomic topics and a similar table in its preface.

| Economic Topics | Recommended Chapters in *The Economics of Macro Issues, 2nd ed.* |
| --- | --- |
| Taxes and Public Spending | 1, 8, 12, 13, 15, 17 |
| Unemployment, Inflation, and Deflation | 6, 7, 8, 9, 10, 11 |
| Measuring the Economy's Performance | 6 |
| Economic Growth and Development | 1, 2, 3, 4, 5 |
| Classical and Keynesian Macro Analyses | 8 |
| Fiscal Policy | 12, 14, 15 |
| Deficits and the Public Debt | 12, 14, 16, 17 |
| Money and Banking | 21 |
| Money Creation and Deposit Insurance | 22 |
| Monetary Policy: Domestic and International | 9, 10, 11, 18, 19 |
| Stabilization and the Global Economy | 6, 7, 9, 10, 11, 14, 18, 19 |
| International Trade | 5, 23, 24, 25, 26 |
| International Finance | 27 |

# Preface

If you were to do a careful review of front-page stories in newspapers over the last few years, you would be struck by the prominence of macroeconomic issues. Indeed, changes in the unemployment rate, inflation, the federal budget deficit, the international balance of payments, interest rates, and Social Security seem to dominate the economic news. These issues also have played a prominent role in recent elections.

What we find surprising is the air of certainty that reporters, politicians, and commentators exhibit when they discuss macroeconomic issues. This is particularly disturbing because, for the most part, macroeconomic discussions in the mass media are not only far from accurate, but in many instances they are dead wrong. Reporters and politicians have been subjected to so many myths about macroeconomic issues over the years that for the most part they have become unable to distinguish the true from the false.

In revising *The Economics of Macro Issues* for this new edition, we have once again sought to help the reader to differentiate the economic way of thinking from speculation, misinformation, and just plain bad reasoning. Here are just a few of the issues that are new for this edition:

- *Outsourcing*—The practice of using foreign workers to perform tasks traditionally undertaken by domestic workers has come under widespread criticism. Politicians and journalists alike have decried the practice, claiming it will lead to rising unemployment and falling real income for Americans. We show that, in fact, outsourcing is not different from other forms of international trade. Hence, its practice can be expected to improve economic performance of the American economy, enriching us and the rest of the world with whom we trade.
- *The stock market*—It is routine to hear stockbrokers, journalists, and so-called financial experts claim that "the market will rise (or fall, or remain unchanged) tomorrow (or next week or next year)," as though they knew something

that you don't. Have no fear: they don't. That's the good
news. But the bad news is that despite your best efforts in
this class or any other, you too are unlikely to beat the market. Although the stock market can be expected to move up
over the long run, its only predictability other than that is
its unpredictability.

• *The trade deficit*—If one were to believe commentators on
this one, then the end of the world is near. Supposedly,
because we are importing more goods and services than we
are exporting, we are "mortgaging the future" and destined
to suffer declining levels of real income and economic
growth. But the doomsayers miss the fact that America is
still the best place in the world for people to invest their
wealth. That foreigners want to invest and lend here in the
United States means that we are able to have lower interest
rates and higher stock prices than would otherwise be the
case. But for this to happen, we must buy something from
them in return; hence the trade deficit: our purchases of
their goods and services give them the cash to invest with
us. The pundits also miss the fact that from the Civil War
until World War I, America's trade patterns with the rest of
the world looked much like they look today—and real
income grew at rates that were high by historical standards.
Do we need to understand the trade deficit? Absolutely; but
we certainly don't need to lose sleep over it.

In general, an analysis of macroeconomic issues requires only
basic economic concepts, ones that are universal across time,
cultures, and economies and can be used in debates about
appropriate national economic policies. The chapters that follow are neither complex nor difficult. Good economics—like all
good science—is simple, and we have subjected our writing to
this same test.

We hope that you have as much fun reading this book as we
had writing it. Both of us have worked on macroeconomic
issues for many years. We continue to do so because we are
optimists. We believe that the more people know how to analyze national economic problems, the greater the chances that
correct policies will be put into effect.

Naturally, in addition to analyzing new issues for this edition of *Macro Issues* we have been through all of the other chapters with a fine-tooth comb, editing and updating them to reflect the very latest in economic theory and economic events. In revising the book, we have been aided greatly by the reviewers of the last edition, who have served as our welcome critics, noting our shortcomings, and suggesting improvements. These reviewers include

Carlos Aguilar, El Paso Community College
Anas Faisal Alhaji, Ohio Northern University
Thomas Birch, University of New Hampshire, Manchester
Adrian Fleissig, California State University, Fullerton
Jim Lee, Texas A&M University, Corpus Christi
Mary Kassis, State University of West Georgia
William Mosher, Clark University
Porntawee Nantamasikarn, University of Hawaii
Robert Seeley, Wilkes University
Jason White, Northwest Missouri State University

In addition, numerous users e-mailed us with helpful suggestions on how we might improve the book. To our reviewers and interested users alike, we offer our greatest thanks.

We wish to thank Sue Jasin of K&M Consulting for her expert typing and editing and Robbie Benjamin for her unstinting demand for clarity of thought and exposition. We also wish to thank our editors at Addison Wesley, Denise Clinton, Roxanne Hoch, and Kirsten Dickinson, for their encouragement and help with this project. Finally, we thank John Orr of Orr Book Services for his expert and rapid production job on this project.

RLM
DKB

# part ONE

## The Miracle of
## Economic Growth

# 1

# *Rich Nation, Poor Nation*

Why do the citizens of some nations grow rich, while the inhabitants of others remain poor? Your initial answer might be, "because of differences in the **natural resource endowments** of the nations." It is surely true that ample endowments of energy, timber, and fertile land all help increase wealth. But natural resources can be only a very small part of the answer, as witnessed by many counterexamples. Switzerland and Luxembourg, for example, are nearly devoid of key natural resources, and yet decade after decade, the real incomes of citizens of those lands have grown rapidly, propelling them to great prosperity. Similarly, Hong Kong, which consists of but a few square miles of rock and hillside, is one of the economic miracles of the last century, while in Russia, a land amply endowed with vast quantities of virtually every important resource, most people remain mired in economic misery.

## Unraveling the Mystery of Growth

A number of recent studies have begun to unravel the mystery of economic growth. Repeatedly, they have found that it is the fundamental political and legal **institutions** of society that are conducive to growth. Of these, political stability, secure private property rights, and legal systems based on the **rule of law** are among the most important. Such institutions encourage people to make long-term investments in improvements to land and in all forms of physical and human capital. These investments raise the **capital stock,** which in turn provides for more growth long into the future. And the cumulative effects of this growth over time eventually yield much higher standards of living.

Professor Paul Mahoney of the University of Virginia, for example, has studied the contrasting effects of different legal systems on economic growth. Many legal systems around the world today are based on one of two basic models: the English **common law system** and the French **civil law system.** Common law systems reflect a conscious decision in favor of a limited role for government and emphasize the importance of the judiciary in constraining the power of the executive and legislative branches of government. In contrast, civil law systems favor the creation of a strong centralized government in which the legislature and the executive branch have the power to grant preferential treatment to special interests. Below, we show a sample of common law and civil law nations:

## Differing Legal Systems

| Common Law Nations | Civil Law Nations |
| --- | --- |
| Australia | Brazil |
| Canada | Egypt |
| India | Germany |
| Israel | Greece |
| New Zealand | Italy |
| United Kingdom | Mexico |
| United States | Sweden |

## The Importance of Secure Property Rights

Mahoney finds that the security of property rights is much stronger in nations with common law systems, such as the United Kingdom and its former colonies, including the United States. In nations such as France and its former colonies, the civil law systems are much more likely to yield unpredictable changes in the rules of the game—the structure of **property and contract rights.** This, in turn, makes people reluctant to make long-term fixed investments in nations with civil law systems, a fact that ultimately slows their growth and lowers the standard of living of their citizens.

The reasoning here is simple. If the police will not help you protect your rights to a home or car, you are less likely to acquire those assets. Similarly, if you cannot easily enforce business or employment contracts that you make, you are much less likely to make those contracts—and thus less likely to produce as many goods or services. Plus, if you cannot plan for the future because you don't know what the rules of the game will be in ten years, or perhaps even one year from now, then you are far less likely to make the productive long-term investments that require years to pay off. Common law systems seem to do a better job at enforcing contracts and securing property rights and, thus, would be expected to promote economic activity now and economic growth over time.

When Mahoney examined the economic performance of nations around the world from 1960 until the 1990s, he found that economic growth has been one-third higher in the common law nations with their strong property rights than it has been in civil law nations. Over the thirty-plus years covered by his study, the standard of living—measured by real per capita income—jumped more than 20 percent in common law nations compared to civil law nations. If such a pattern persisted over the span of a century, it would produce a staggering 80 percent real-per-capita-income differential in favor of nations with secure property rights.

## Other Institutions Are Important Too

Recently, economists William Easterly and Ross Levine have taken a much broader view, both across time and across institutions, assessing the economic growth of a variety of nations since their days as colonies. These authors examine how institutions such as political stability, protection of persons and property against violence or theft, security of contracts, and freedom from regulatory burdens all contribute to sustained economic growth. They find that it is key institutions such as these, rather than natural resource endowments, that explain long-term differences in growth and thus present-day differences in levels of real income. To illustrate the powerful effect of institutions, consider the contrast between Mexico, with a real per capita income of about $9,400 today, and the United States, with a real per capita income of about $38,200. Easterly and Levine conclude that if Mexico had developed with the same political and legal institutions that the United States has enjoyed, per capita income in Mexico today would be *equal* to that in the United States!

## The Historical Roots of Today's Institutions

In light of the tremendous importance of institutions in determining long-term growth, Easterly and Levine go on to ask another important question: How have countries gotten the political and legal institutions they have today? The answer has to do with disease, of all things. The seventy-two countries examined by Easterly and Levine are all former European colonies, where a variety of colonial strategies were pursued. In Australia, New Zealand, and North America, the colonists found geography and climate that were conducive to good health. Permanent settlement in such locations was attractive, and so the settlers created institutions to protect private property and curb the power of the state. But when Europeans arrived in Africa and South America, they encountered tropical diseases—such as malaria and yellow fever—that produced high mortality among the settlers. This discouraged permanent settlement and encouraged a mentality focused on extracting metals, cash crops, and other resources. This, in turn, provided little incentive to promote democratic institutions or stable long-term property rights systems. The differing initial institutions helped shape economic growth over the years, and their persistence continues to shape the political and legal character and the standard of living in these nations today.

## No Property Rights Means No Property

Recent events also illustrate that the effects of political and legal institutions can be drastically accelerated—at least in the wrong direction. When Zimbabwe won its independence from Great Britain in 1980, it was one of the most prosperous nations in Africa. Soon after taking power as Zimbabwe's first (and thus far only) president, Robert Mugabe began disassembling that nation's rule of law, tearing apart the institutions that had helped it grow rich. He reduced the security of property rights in land and eventually confiscated those rights altogether. Mugabe also has gradually taken control of the prices of most goods and services in his nation and even controls the price of its national currency, at least the price at which Zimbabweans are allowed to trade it. The Mugabe government has also confiscated large stocks of food and much of the value of anything that might be exported out of or imported into Zimbabwe. In short, anything that is produced or saved has become subject to confiscation, so the incentives to do either are—to put it mildly—reduced. As a result, between 1980 and 1996, real per capita income in Zimbabwe fell by one-third, and since 1996 it has fallen by an additional one-third. Unemployment is rampant, investment nonexistent, and since 2002 the inflation rate in Zimbabwe has averaged 400 percent per year. In only twenty-five years, the fruit of many decades of labor and capital investment has been destroyed, because the very institutions that made that fruit possible have been eliminated. It is a lesson we ignore at our peril.

## For Critical Analysis

1. Consider two countries, A and B, and suppose that both have identical *physical* endowments of, say, iron ore. But in country A, any profits that are made from mining the ore are subject to confiscation by the government of A, while in country B, there is no such risk. How does the risk of expropriation affect the *economic* endowments of the two nations? In which nation are people richer?

2. In light of your answer to the previous question, how do you explain the fact that in some countries there is widespread political support for government policies that expropriate resources from some groups for the purpose of handing them out to other groups?

3. Going to college in the United States raises average lifetime earnings by about two-thirds—given our current political and economic institutions. But suppose that the ownership of the added income created by your college education suddenly became uncertain. Specifically, suppose a law was passed in your state that enabled the governor to (i) select 10 percent of the graduating class from all of the state's colleges and universities each year and (ii) impose a tax of up to 50 percent on the difference between the earnings of these people in their first job and the average earnings of people in the state who have only a high school education. What would happen to immigration into or out of the state? What would happen to attendance at colleges and universities within the state? If the governor were allowed to arbitrarily decide who got hit with the new tax, what would happen to campaign contributions to the governor? What would happen to the number of people "volunteering" to work in the governor's next campaign? Would your decision to invest in a college education change?

# Return of the Luddites: Technophobia and Economic Growth

In March 1811, General Ned Ludd and his Army of Redressers began the attacks. The objects of their rage were factories in Nottingham, England that were using newly installed weaving machines. The **"Luddites,"** as they came to be known, feared that the new machines would take away their jobs and leave them unemployed. Passage of the Frame Breaking Act (which specified the death penalty for anyone who destroyed industrial machinery) soon brought a halt to the Luddites' activities. But their spirit is resurgent today in those people who see catastrophe in every new technology.

## Technology and Wealth

There is no doubt that technological advances have fueled economic growth and thereby markedly improved the lives and lengthened the life spans of human beings. Whether we look at the wheel, which drastically reduces transportation costs, or vaccines and antibiotics, which save the lives of millions of people every year, technology has raised our **wealth.** Higher wealth, in turn, enables us to make a broader range of decisions over the usage of a wider range of resources. People who are wealthy can choose to have improved health for their children or higher environmental quality, or—if they are wealthy enough—both. People who are poor must watch their offspring die of preventable childhood diseases, are powerless to improve the environmental conditions in which they live, and face the prospect of never doing anything about either outcome. It is no accident that the residents of technologically advanced nations have longer life spans; they live longer because the technology has raised their wealth and enabled them to choose more healthful diets and higher-quality health care. Likewise, it is no accident that the average life span around the world rose to sixty-seven years from thirty during the twentieth century. This occurred because the spread of technology raised wealth and enabled people to make life-preserving and health-enhancing choices that simply were not feasible in 1900. And note finally that higher wealth—spurred by technological advances—has enabled us to choose better outcomes everywhere in our lives, including education, environmental quality, cultural amenities, charitable activities, and so forth.

To be sure, not *every* technological advance has made us unambiguously better off. Nuclear weapons, for example, have threatened human survival since their invention. More recently, improved knowledge of how to refine anthrax spores has been used to kill people and poses the possibility of killing still more. Nevertheless, on balance the overwhelming impact of technological advance has been to spur economic growth and, in so doing, vastly improve the economic condition of humankind.

Despite the huge benefits created by technological advances, many people in addition to Ned Ludd's Army of Redressers have objected to the introduction of new technology. Because these objections are both persistent and loudly voiced, it is important that we examine them carefully to assess their validity.

## The Fear of Competition

The Luddites' actions were driven by one motive, pure and simple: they were hand weavers who objected to the competition offered by the new mechanized weaving machines of the day. They perceived, quite correctly, that the new machines would reduce the demand for hand weavers, and so they attempted to prevent this competition. But the new technology did more than compel many hand weavers to learn how to use the machines or to find employment in other pursuits. It also drastically reduced the price of textiles, enabling people to own more than one set of clothes, worn all day, every day—a "luxury" that reduced deaths from cold weather in the winter and hot weather in the summer. Moreover, the rapid spread of the textile industry helped spur the development of other technology that led to the creation of new industries, such as chemicals, which have further raised our wealth. To be sure, the hand weavers were worse off, but the gains then and later to the rest of society have been staggeringly greater.

In more recent times, the fear of competition has spurred numerous other objections to technological advances. For example, when vegetable-oil-based margarine was invented around the middle of the twentieth century, the dairy industry claimed that the new product was a threat to human health (this from the purveyors of animal-fat-based butter!), and a fraud as well, because the new stuff was made to look like butter. Dairy lobbyists were successful in persuading many state legislatures to outlaw yellow margarine, forcing consumers to take home white margarine from the store and mix it with yellow food coloring in their own kitchens. The substantially lower price of the new product was enough to overcome dairy industry resistance, however, and margarine became a commercial success long before the health *benefits* of vegetable oil over animal fat became apparent.

Somewhat later in the twentieth century, the development of electronic typesetting offered competition for Linotype machines, which required skilled workers to set metal type before newspapers and books could be printed. The first of these electronic typesetters, called the Photon, was four times as fast as the Linotype and could be operated by lower-wage clerical workers, rather than by expensive members of the International Typographical Union (ITU). The competitive threat posed by the Photon led the ITU to call a four-month strike against all New York City newspapers in 1962–1963. The strike ended the life of the *New York Mirror*, but the remaining newspapers won from the union the right to use the Photon—in return for guaranteeing all existing ITU typesetters lifetime employment contracts. The new machines drastically reduced the costs of printing newspapers, books, and so forth, thereby raising society's wealth. Within a few decades, of course, the Photons themselves were made obsolete by yet another technological advance, the relatively low-cost, but high-powered, personal computer—a development no doubt objected to by Photon operators.

## The Fear of Adverse Effects

It has become commonplace in recent years to object to specific new technology on the grounds that it has or *might* have adverse effects on human, animal, or plant life. This, for example, is the source of current objections to irradiated food and to genetically modified food.

This type of objection stems largely from scares over DDT and other pesticides, which developed during the 1960s. It was claimed, for example, that DDT caused cancer in humans and thus should be banned. Despite the claims of dangers to humans, the World Health Organization has found that "the only confirmed cases of injury have been the result of massive accidental or suicidal ingestion." Moreover, the use of DDT was enormously successful in wiping out malaria in underdeveloped nations around the world, saving the lives of millions of people. DDT even significantly cut the costs of raising fruits and vegetables, thereby increasing the consumption of these important cancer-*fighting* foodstuffs. Despite the evidence, however, most countries have banned DDT. The result has been a resurgence of malaria, the deaths of millions of those living in tropical climates, and an unequivocal threat to the lives of hundreds of millions of other human beings.

On the other side of the coin, there is evidence that indiscriminate use of DDT threatened the health and existence of numerous animal species, including the bald eagle. It is perhaps instructive, though, that recent research reveals that this harm to animal life resulted from excessive applications of DDT, that government agencies (rather than farmers) were responsible for almost all such applications, and that if the government agencies had followed the manufacturers' instructions, it is likely that no animal species would ever have been threatened.

## The Fear of Wealth

Strange as it may seem, the third objection to technological advances is that they stimulate economic growth and make us richer! There are two complaints here. First, there is the argument that economic growth promotes population growth, which will eventually overwhelm our supposedly fixed resource base and thereby lead to widespread starvation and misery. Second, there is the claim that economic growth inevitably leads to environmental degradation, which in turn threatens the existence not only of humans, but of all species. Whatever the plausibility of these arguments to some, the evidence clearly refutes these notions.

Technological advances that raise our wealth *do* tend to promote population growth. After all, it takes resources to live. But the positive effect of wealth on population is much less than you might think because as people get richer, they tend to have fewer children per family. Instead of pouring resources into a larger number of children, they put those resources into a higher-quality experience for the fewer children that they do rear, for example, by spending more funds on education. More importantly, a crucial way that technological advances raise our wealth is by enabling us to extract resources more effectively and to use those resources more efficiently. Just consider some seemingly mundane examples:

- Steam injection wells permit more complete extraction of petroleum.
- Improved machinery and designs have cut the weight of aluminum beverage cans by 40 percent.
- Advances in chemistry have created stronger, lighter plastics and longer-lasting paints and finishes.

As the result of these and thousands of other inventions, the world's reserves of oil, natural gas, aluminum, zinc, and many other commodities have *risen* over time, despite our continued use of these resources. So, to be concerned that growing prosperity will cause population growth that outstrips our resources is to fail to understand the sources of that growing prosperity.

But what impact does higher wealth have on the environment? After all, more consumption necessitates more production, and that, it seems, must lead to more pollution. This reasoning would be correct if it did not ignore two crucial facts. Technological advances do help promote production, but they make it possible to produce goods with fewer inputs per unit of output, and they also make possible the development of cleaner processes, such as hybrid cars and solar power. Moreover, although early stages of economic development are often accompanied by environmental degradation, the effect is soon overwhelmed by another one. Environmental quality is a **normal good,** that is, a good that people want to consume more of as they get richer. The result is that soon after technological advances begin pushing up incomes, people begin insisting that more and more resources be devoted to protecting and enhancing environmental amenities. Indeed, after per capita income reaches about $5,000 in any country, environmental quality begins improving dramatically as incomes rise more. Thus, technological advances don't merely bring us lighter beverage cans; they ultimately bring us a better environment.

## The Bottom Line

The lesson of history—emphatically and unmistakably—is that technological change raises our wealth and improves the lot of humankind. Surely, there is always the *possibility* that some new technology could, on balance, cause more harm than good. But if we know anything at all, it is that systematic attempts to suppress technological change almost *always* cause more harm than good. It is sensible to consider carefully the potential adverse effects of new technologies and to make sure that all of the costs of those technologies are taken into account. But it is foolhardy—and impoverishing—to let unfounded fears blind us to the benefits of those technologies.

## For Critical Analysis

1. If we want to obtain the maximum possible good for humankind, why is it important to take into account both the benefits and the costs of new technology, rather than simply focusing on one or the other?

2. Some people argue that a special government agency should assess, pass judgment on, and either permit or prevent the introduction of all new technological advances. Are there any reasons to think a government agency would do a better job at this (that is, benefit humankind more) than the private-sector inventors of those technologies? Are there any reasons to think such a government agency would do an inferior job?

3. Analyze the economic consequences of outlawing the wheel, which was, after all, a major technological innovation. First, select some specific markets and see how making the wheel illegal would (i) affect the demand and supply, and (ii) affect the economic well-being of producers and consumers in those markets. Second, consider the economy as a whole: Is the level of real income likely to be higher or lower as a result of abolishing the wheel? How does the wheel differ from other major technological innovations, in the past or present?

# 3

# The Dragon and the Tigers: Economic Growth in Asia

Back in the 1980s, a select group of economies in Asia came to be known as the "Asian tigers" because of their aggressive approach to economic growth. Included among the tigers were Singapore, Malaysia, Thailand, and Indonesia. All took the view that a combination of low wages and high export sales represented the fast track to economic growth and prosperity. Now, these tigers are being overtaken by the "dragon" of Asia—China—which is following the same path, with perhaps even more success.

## The Guangdong Experiment

For decades after the Communists' rise to power in 1949, China was best known for poverty and repression, and its aggression came mostly on the military front. But in recent years *economic* aggression has become the Chinese byword. Although both poverty and repression are still the norm, both are changing for the better. China, it seems, is trying to learn from capitalism, even if not converting to it.

16

China's economic offensive began about twenty-five years ago in its southeastern province of Guangdong. The Chinese leadership decided to use this province as a test case to see if capitalist **direct foreign investment** could stimulate **economic growth** in a way that could be politically controlled. The experience was deemed a success—economic growth soared amid political stability. What the government learned from the experience helped it smooth the 1997 transition of Hong Kong from British to Chinese control. Most important in terms of China's long-term economic aspirations, many foreign investors came to view the Guangdong experiment as solid evidence that they could invest in China without fear that the Communist government would confiscate their capital. Around 1992, foreign investment began to flow into China. Today, the annual rate of such investment is nearly ten times greater than it was at the beginning of the 1990s.

## That Same Old Song: Demand and Supply

Economic investment is being attracted to China by two powerful forces: **demand** and **supply.** On the demand side, 1.3 billion people live there, some 20 percent of the world's population. Although **per capita income** is still low by world standards, it has been growing by about 7 to 8 percent per year, after adjusting for inflation. At that rate, the standard of living for the Chinese people—and thus their **purchasing power** in world markets—is doubling every nine years or so. China is already the world's largest cell phone market, with 200 million customers. It is estimated that within a few years China will account for 20 percent of the world's purchases of personal computers. Indeed, China now spends $50 billion per year on information technology and services, and this amount is growing at a rate of about 25 percent per year. Sometime in the next 20 to 30 years, the Chinese economy will almost surely supplant the U.S. economy as the world's largest.

With its population of 1.3 billion individuals, China also offers attractions on the supply side. Although U.S. and European firms with operations in China choose to pay their workers considerably more than state-owned enterprises pay, labor is still relatively inexpensive. Manufacturing and production workers employed by U.S. or European firms, for example, earn under $4 per hour, only about one-fourth what the foreign firms would have to pay in their home markets. And when it comes to highly skilled workers, the Chinese labor market is even more attractive. China's universities produce more than 450,000 engineering graduates each year, including 50,000 in computer science. (By comparison, the United States produces about 30,000 new computer science graduates each year.) Most importantly, firms can hire those engineers for salaries that are only 10 to 20 percent of the cost of hiring engineers in the United States or Europe.

Furthermore, particularly in the cities, the Chinese workforce is generally well educated and English-speaking, making China even more attractive to foreign employers. Collaborative scientific ventures between Chinese researchers and U.S. firms are becoming increasingly common. A research team at Beijing University played a role in deciphering the genetic makeup of rice, for example. American computer hardware and software firms including Intel, IBM, Oracle, and Microsoft have shifted some key components of their research to China in recent years. American firms are even setting up customer service call centers in China. When Microsoft customers in the United States call in for help, they may well find themselves talking with one of that company's 400 engineers who are located in Shanghai.

## A Tale of the Tablet

Not long ago computer makers began offering what has become one of the hot-selling items of recent years, the tablet PC, equipped with software that reads handwriting. The development of the software used by the tablet PC illustrates the key elements of China's recent growth.

The Chinese language has thousands of individual characters and no alphabet. As a result, the language cannot be easily accommodated on computer keyboards. This problem significantly slowed sales of computer hardware and software in China during the 1980s and 1990s. In the hopes of tapping the huge Chinese market, Microsoft established a major research lab in Beijing, China's capital, with the goal of making computers easier for the Chinese to use. For more than a year, researchers fed a computer a steady stream of handwritten documents, including notes, diagrams, and even shopping lists. Gradually, after many hours of human programming and learning-by-doing on the part of the computer, the Chinese researchers developed a program that could distinguish words from everything else and then turn the words into typed text. What worked for handwriting in China would work for handwriting anywhere. Equipped with this software, a viable tablet PC was born.

Both elements of China's growth—demand and supply— were clearly at work in this process. Without the huge potential market in China, this project wouldn't have been given priority and might not have been undertaken at all. Moreover, without well-trained, English-speaking Chinese computer scientists at the heart of the project, it is unlikely that Microsoft could have been successful. The upshot of the project is that a product whose primary impetus came from China is yielding benefits around the world, and making the computer market in China even more alluring to U.S. firms.

## The Tigers Are Worried

China's rapid economic expansion has caused a huge increase in its demand for raw materials and other inputs, many of which are being supplied by Malaysia, Thailand, and Singapore. Although these Asian tigers are grateful for the boom in exports, they are also concerned by the growing competition they face from their neighbor to the north. Chinese medium- and high-tech industries are starting to cut into the market share of the very sectors that have helped fuel the growth of the Asian tigers over the past twenty-five years. The situation is even more critical in Japan: wages are much higher there than in China, but the Japanese technological lead over China is gradually eroding. "Are we to become a vassal of the Chinese dynasty again?" asked one Japanese official, clearly concerned that his nation's manufacturing firms were having trouble competing with Chinese firms.

Although lower wages among the tigers are keeping them competitive for now, they are concerned about the future, because competition for foreign investment is particularly intense. China's 2001 entry into the **World Trade Organization** prompted a surge in foreign investment there, even as China's rivals in the region saw their foreign investment shrink. Without fresh outside capital, the economies of Malaysia, Singapore, and Thailand may all start looking like Japan's, where growth has been essentially zero since the mid-1990s and unemployment is a chronic problem. Eventually, Japan as well as China's other neighbors will adjust to the growing economic presence of China, but the transition may be unpleasant.

## What Does the Future Hold?

As we saw in Chapter 1, political and legal **institutions** are crucial foundations for sustained economic growth. Despite China's advances over the last twenty-five years, its future may be clouded unless it can successfully deal with two crucial institutional issues.

First, there is the matter of resolving the tension inherent when a Communist dictatorship tries to use capitalism as the engine of economic growth. Capitalism thrives best in an environment of freedom, and itself creates an awareness of and appreciation for the benefits of that freedom. Yet freedom is antithetical to the ideological and political tenets of the Communist government of China. Will the government be tempted to confiscate the fruits of capitalist success to support itself? Or will growing pressure for more political freedom force the government to repress the capitalist system to protect itself? Either route would likely bring economic growth to a swift halt in China.

The second potential long-term problem involves China's cultural attitude toward intellectual property. In a land where imitation is viewed as the sincerest form of flattery, people routinely utilize the ideas of others in their own pursuits. As a result, patent and copyright laws in China are far weaker than in Western nations. Moreover, actions elsewhere considered to be commercial theft (such as software piracy) are largely tolerated in China. If foreign firms find they cannot protect their economic assets in the Chinese market, foreign investment will suffer accordingly, and so, too, will the growing dragon that depends so heavily on it.

## For Critical Analysis

1. Currently, AIDS is spreading rapidly in China, largely as a result of contaminated blood supplies. If the government fails to stop the spread of AIDS, what are the likely consequences for future economic growth in China?
2. In 1989, a massive protest against political repression in China was halted by the government's massacre of more than 150 individuals at Tiananmen Square in Beijing. What impact do you think that episode had on foreign investment and growth in China during the years immediately after the episode?
3. Presumably, the residents of China are consumers of goods as well as producers of them. Hence, as growth takes place in China, not only will the worldwide supply of some goods increase, so, too, will the worldwide demand for other goods. What impact will Chinese economic growth have on the prices of the goods it supplies on world markets, relative to the goods it demands on world markets? Do *all* producers of goods in foreign nations lose as a result of Chinese economic growth? Do *all* consumers in foreign nations gain as a result of China's economic growth?

# 4

# *Immigrants and Economic Growth*

Nobody can deny that the United States is a land of immigrants. Should anyone try, simply point them in the direction of the Statue of Liberty, a gift from the citizens of France in recognition of America's role as a haven for "tired . . . poor . . . huddled masses yearning to breathe free." Yet both before and after the statue's 1886 dedication, the immigration that it celebrates has had a darker side, for not everyone who comes to the United States does so legally. This nation has always had a flow of illegal aliens, also known as **undocumented aliens.** Many of these individuals are tourists who overstay their visas and start working. Many are from Mexico and other Latin American countries. The Census Bureau estimates that about eight million illegal aliens now live in the United States permanently, with another 350,000 arriving each year. But no one, not even the Census Bureau, knows for sure how many there are. Some observers argue that as many as twelve million illegal aliens may reside in the United States, with a million or more coming in each year.

## The Legislation of Immigration

Periodically, the federal government has attempted to reduce illegal immigration. The Immigration Reform and Control Act of 1986, for example, imposed severe penalties on employers who willfully hire illegal aliens (with fines ranging from $250 to $10,000 for each offense). Employers who repeatedly violate this law can be jailed for up to six months.

The 1986 law also included an **amnesty** program. From the summer of 1987 to the summer of 1988, illegal aliens who could prove that they had been in this country continuously for at least five years could apply to obtain temporary legal residency status. Eighteen months later, they could apply for permanent residency. Eventually, they could apply for citizenship.

The most recent legislation attempting to stem illegal immigration was the 1996 Immigration Reform Act, but immigration policy remains the focus of a continuing debate in the United States. Many Americans strongly believe that immigrants, especially illegal immigrants, take jobs that U.S. citizens would otherwise have and thereby lower Americans' wages. These critics also fear that new waves of immigrants will have difficulty fitting in with present-day U.S. society.

Supporters of immigration point out the obvious: at one time or another, all of us were immigrants (even Native Americans, whose ancestors are believed to have come in over the Siberian land bridge many thousands of years ago). Immigration has made the United States what it is today. Therefore, ask immigration advocates, how can we arbitrarily decide that immigration today is "bad" for America? Today, just as in 1886 and before, many new immigrants start on the first rung of the economic ladder by taking the low-paying jobs deemed least attractive by existing Americans. Moreover, now as before, most immigrants pay taxes and adjust rapidly to the requirements of life in their new country.

## The Economics of Immigration

From the point of view of a potential immigrant (or emigrant, as viewed from his or her country of origin), there is an implicit economic equation: those who wish to come to the United States presumably believe that the economic benefits outweigh the economic costs. These costs are significant. They include the cost of travel, the cost of learning a new language for those who do not already speak English, and the cost of giving up whatever degree of social and economic certainty exists in the immigrant's country of origin to face huge uncertainty in a new country. For many who attempt legal immigration, there can be substantial bureaucratic hurdles and high legal costs. The latter costs bulk particularly large when considered relative to the average annual income in the immigrant's country of origin. Finally, of course, there is the often-considerable noneconomic cost of leaving one's family and friends for a far-away land.

On the positive side, the expected economic benefits of immigration equal the net lifetime expected increase in income compared to what one could make in one's country of origin. In addition, of course, there is the little matter of freedom—which we take for granted, but which is often the beacon that burns brightest for the potential newcomer to our shores. Clearly, the continuing flow of immigration informs us that the benefits of emigrating to the United States have outweighed the costs for literally millions and millions of people from other countries. Whether the motive is economic or not for any given immigrant, the package offered by America has been sufficiently attractive that our reputation as the land of immigrants is amply justified.

## The Link between Immigration and U.S. Economic Growth

Imagine you are doing a survey. You stop typical men and women in the street and ask the following question: If we admit more immigrants, will the United States be better off, worse off, or about the same? Similar questions have been asked in numerous opinion polls. As you might expect, the majority of U.S. residents today often answer that more immigration will make the United States worse off. Their reasoning is simple: Most often, they argue that immigrants take jobs away from U.S. residents. Moreover, they say, immigrants are a "drain on the system" in that they use government services without paying their fair share.

The reality has been largely the opposite, though, even over the last decade and a half when the debate over immigration has been so heated. From 1990 to 2004, some fifteen million immigrants entered the United States. Of those fifteen million, almost ten million joined the labor force. Indeed, the Center for Labor Market Studies at Northeastern University discovered that during the 1990s and early 2000s, over 50 percent of new wage earners who joined the labor force were immigrants. Even more striking, eight of ten new male workers during the 1990s were newly arrived immigrants. In contrast, during the 1980s, immigrants accounted for 25 percent of labor force growth, and during the 1970s, they accounted for only 10 percent.

Despite what the opponents of immigration would have you believe, this influx of newcomers was associated with more, not less, economic vitality. When we look at economic growth during the 1990s, we find that it averaged 3.2 percent per year—higher than in a typical decade and higher than in the 1970s and 1980s, when growth averaged between 2.8 and 2.9 percent per year. Just as important, during the 1990s, immigrants prevented population loss in many cities and rural areas and reduced what would have been far greater losses in other areas of the country.

## We Would Have Been Worse Off without So Many Immigrants

According to the Center for Labor Market Studies, the rate of U.S. economic growth would have been lower in the 1990s and early 2000s had there not been so many immigrants. Moreover, the authors of the study discovered that immigrants contribute more in taxes than they use in services. This pattern is particularly true for illegal immigrants, who are unable to avail themselves of any social services offered by local, state, or federal governments. Consequently, when they work, they typically pay taxes and receive few, if any, government services in return. Moreover, illegal immigrants are ineligible for Social Security and other benefits if they stay in the United States.

It is true that immigrants are more likely to collect cash and noncash welfare benefits than are native residents of the United States. Much of the difference in welfare receipt rates is attributable to two groups of immigrants: political refugees (such as from the former Soviet Union), and immigrants who are very young or elderly. Receipt of Medicaid assistance and enrollment in subsidized school lunch programs, for example, are significantly higher among immigrants than among native residents. But, as suggested by the employment figures noted above, most working-age immigrants generally find employment quickly, and contribute substantially to the nation's economic well being.

We also know from prior studies that immigrants lower the wages of existing workers only modestly. Instead, they chiefly take the unskilled low-paying jobs that existing Americans refuse to take at existing wages. This is precisely the pattern that has been observed at least since the early nineteenth century in America. This year's wave of immigrants steps into the shoes of last year's wave, who, in turn, move up to fill the shoes of those who came in the year before. It is a process that fuels economic growth and prosperity throughout the country.

## Immigration after 9/11

Both the domestic and the international press have provided numerous accounts of how the Immigration and Naturalization Service has cracked down on both legal and illegal immigration into the United States since the terrorist attacks of September 2001. According to the Center for Immigration Studies in Washington, D.C., however, in spite of the purported crackdown on immigration, the pace of immigration into the United States has barely slowed. Indeed, the Census Bureau notes that since the census was taken in 2000, roughly three million additional immigrants have arrived in the United States.

So, it would appear that immigration, as always, is here to stay in the United States. As long as labor markets are free to adjust to changing conditions, this country can continue to absorb immigrants with few negative consequences. In fact, if what has happened since 1990 is any indication, more immigration will make the United States in general better off, not worse off— which is surely good news for current and prospective Americans alike.

## For Critical Analysis

1. Why do many labor union leaders argue in favor of restricting immigration?
2. Does it matter whether a potential immigrant wishes to emigrate to the United States for political reasons—to avoid repression at home—or for economic reasons? In other words, is the effect on our economy different depending on a potential immigrant's motivation for coming to live and work in the United States?
3. What is the impact of immigration on the supply of labor in (i) the immigrants' originating countries, and (ii) their destination country? Is it possible that immigration could leave wage rates in the originating and destination countries unchanged? More generally, what would you expect to happen to wages in the destination country relative to wages in the home country, as a result of the immigration? What impact would this have on employment among existing workers in the destination country?

# 5

# *Outsourcing and Economic Growth*

CNN business commentator Lou Dobbs keeps a "hit list" of corporations that send jobs overseas. Such actions are decidedly un-American, Dobbs opines, whenever he gets a chance to express his negative views against **outsourcing.** John Kerry had a name for heads of companies that outsourced telemarketing projects, customer services, and other white-collar jobs to foreign countries: he called them "Benedict Arnold CEOs."

In 2004, Congress tried to pass a bill to prevent any type of outsourcing by the Department of State and the Department of Defense. Republican representative Don Manzullo of Illinois said, "You can't just continue to outsource overseas time after time after time, lose your strategic military base, and then expect this Congress to sit back and see the jobs lost and do nothing." When an advisor to President George W. Bush publicly stated that the foreign outsourcing of service jobs was not such a bad idea, Kerry, as well as numerous other politicians, lambasted the Bush administration for even the suggestion that outsourcing could be viewed in a positive light.

## What Is This "Outsourcing"?

The concept of outsourcing is straightforward: Instead of hiring American workers at home, American corporations hire foreign workers to do the same jobs. As just one example, some of these foreign workers are in India and they do call-center work, answering technical questions for computer purchasers. Another job such workers do well (and cheaply) is software development and debugging. Because of low-cost communication, especially over the Internet, software programmers can be just about anywhere in the world and still work for U. S. corporations.

Besides the fear that outsourcing "robs Americans of jobs," there is also a claim that outsourcing reduces economic growth in the United States. (Presumably, that must mean that it increases economic growth in, say, India.) Because outsourcing is part and parcel of international trade in goods and services, the real question becomes "Can the United States have higher growth rates if it restricts American corporations from 'sending jobs abroad'?"

As we set out to answer this question, it is important to keep one simple fact in mind: outsourcing is nothing more and nothing less than the purchase of labor services from the residents of a foreign nation. When the Detroit Red Wings host the Vancouver Canucks, fans at the game are outsourcing: they are purchasing labor services from Canadians. In this sense, Canadian hockey players are no different from Indian software engineers; they are citizens of foreign nations who are competing with citizens of the United States in the supply of labor services. Just as important, outsourcing is no different from any other form of international trade.

## The Link between Economic Growth and Outsourcing

International trade has been around for thousands of years. That means that the concept of outsourcing certainly is not new, even though the term seems to be. After all, the exchange of services between countries is a part of international trade. In any event, if we decide to restrict this type of international trade in services, we will be restricting international trade in general. Those who study economic growth today have found that the openness of an economy is a key determinant of its rate of economic growth. Any restriction on outsourcing is a type of trade barrier, one that will reduce the benefits we obtain from international trade.

There is a clear historical link between economic growth and trade barriers. Look at Figure 5-1. There you see the relationship between the openness of an economy—fewer or more trade barriers—and the rate of economic growth. On the bottom of this graph is a trade barrier index, which for the United States is equal to 100. On the vertical axis you see the average annual growth of income per capita in percentage terms.

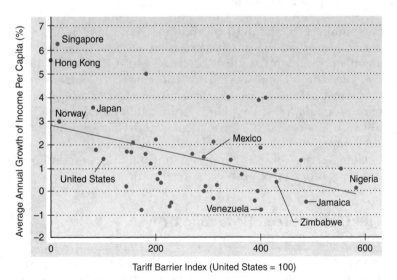

**Figure 5-1. Relationship Between Economic Growth and Barriers to International Trade**

It is evident from this graph that those countries that have fewer international trade barriers have also had higher rates of economic growth. The lesson of history (and as we shall see in Section V, the lesson of economics) is quite clear: international trade raises economic growth, and this, in turn, raises economic well-being. Government efforts to restrict outsourcing will restrict international trade, and this, in turn, will make Americans poorer, not richer.

## Will the U.S. Become a Third World Country?

In spite of the evidence just shown, Paul Craig Roberts, a former Reagan administration treasury official, declared at a Brookings Institution conference that "The United States will be a third world country in twenty years." His prediction was based on the idea that entire classes of high-wage service sector employees will eventually find themselves in competition with highly skilled workers abroad who earn much less than their U.S. counterparts. He contended that U.S. software programmers and radiologists, for example, will not be able to compete in the global economy. Thus, he argued, the United States will lose millions of white-collar jobs due to outsourcing of service sector employment to India and China.

Jeffrey E. Garden, dean of the Yale School of Management, reiterated and expanded on this prediction. He believes that the transfer of jobs abroad will accelerate for generations to come. He argues that in countries from China to the Czech Republic there is a "virtually unlimited supply of industrious and educated labor working at a fraction of U.S. wages." Similarly, according to Craig Barrett, chief executive of the chip maker Intel, American workers today face the prospect of "300 million well-educated people in India, China, and Russia who can do effectively any job that can be done in the U.S."

Still other commentators have claimed that India alone will soak up three to four million jobs from the U.S. labor market by 2015. Some even believe that this number may exceed ten million. If true, one might expect American software developers and call-center technicians to start moving to India!

## Some Overlooked Facts

Much of the outsourcing discussion has ignored two simple facts that turn out to be important if we really want to understand what the future will bring.

- *Outsourcing is the result of trade liberalization in foreign nations:* After decades (and even longer) of isolation, the markets in China, India, and Eastern Europe have begun to open up to international trade. As is often the case when governments finally allow their people to trade internationally, these governments have pushed hard to stimulate exports—of labor services as well as goods. But this cannot be a long-term equilibrium strategy, because the workers producing those goods and supplying those services are doing it because they want to become consumers. Soon enough, and this is already happening, they want to spend their hard-earned money on goods and services, many of which are produced abroad. Thus, today's outsourcing of jobs to those nations must eventually turn into exports of goods and services to those same nations.
- *Prices adjust to keep markets in balance:* The supply curve of labor is upward-sloping. Thus, as U.S. corporations hire foreign workers (either directly by outsourcing, or indirectly by importing goods) market wages in foreign lands must rise. Between 2003 and 2004, for example, Indian labor-outsourcing companies saw wages rise almost 20 percent. Over a longer span, real wages in southern China (which has been open to trade far longer than India), are now *six times higher* than they were just twenty years ago. Such wage adjustments obviously reduce the attractiveness of foreign suppliers. Moreover, it is not just wages that adjust: the relative values of national currencies move, too. Between 2003 and 2004, the value of the dollar fell more than 20 percent, making foreign goods (and workers) more expensive here, and making U.S. goods and workers more attractive in foreign markets.

None of these adjustments are instantaneous. Moreover, they are occurring because some American firms are moving output and employment abroad; hence, at least some U.S. workers are having to move to lower-paying jobs, often with a spell of unemployment along the way. How big is the impact in the short run, before all of the price adjustments take place? According to the Bureau of Labor Statistics, in 2003 some 3.3 percent of the 1.2 million workers displaced due to extended mass layoffs lost their jobs because of import competition; of this, only one percentage point was the result of outsourcing. The impact of outsourcing in 2004 was even smaller. So, if you are currently a U.S. software developer, you don't have to worry about packing your bags for Bombay, at least not soon.

## Don't Forget Foreign Firms' Insourcing

U.S. firms are not the only ones that engage in outsourcing. Many foreign firms do the same. When a foreign firm outsources to the United States, we can call it **insourcing.** For example, Mexican firms routinely send data to U.S. accounting businesses for calculation of payrolls and for maintaining financial records. Many foreign hospitals pay our radiologists to read X-rays and MRI images. Foreign firms use American firms to do a host of other services, many of which involve consulting. Also, when a foreign automobile manufacturer builds an assembly plant in the United States, it is, in effect, outsourcing automobile assembly to American workers. Thus, American workers in the South Carolina BMW plant, the Alabama Mercedes-Benz plant, or the Toyota or Honda plants located in Tennessee and Ohio are all beneficiaries of the fact that those foreign companies have outsourced jobs to the United States. Indeed, all across the country and around the world, hundreds of millions of workers are employed by "foreign" corporations—although in most cases, it's getting difficult to tell the nationality of any company, given the far-flung nature of today's global enterprises.

## What Really Matters Is the Long Run

If you own the only grocery store in your small town, you are clearly harmed if a competing store opens across the street. If you work in a small telephone equipment store and a large company starts taking away business via Internet sales, you will obviously be worse off. If you used to be employed at a call center for customer service at Wal-Mart and have just lost your job because Wal-Mart outsourced to a cheaper Indian firm, you will have to look for a new job.

These kinds of "losses" of income or jobs have occurred since the beginning of commerce. They will always exist in any dynamic economy. Indeed, if we look over the American economy as a whole, roughly *one million workers lose their jobs every week*. But slightly *more* than one million people find a new job every week. So, on balance, employment in the United States keeps growing, even though the average person will change jobs every three years—some of them no doubt because of international competition. But job turnover like this is an essential component of a labor market that is continually adjusting to economic change. It is a sign of health, not sickness, in the economy. If you find this hard to believe, you can look west or east. In Japan, efforts to "protect" workers from international trade resulted in economic stagnation and depressed real income growth from 1989 to 2004. In Europe, similar efforts to "preserve" the jobs of existing workers have resulted in *higher*, not lower unemployment, because firms are unwilling to hire people that they cannot fire later.

If you are still wondering, simply look back at Figure 5-1, or ahead to Section V of this book. The lessons of history and of economics are clear: Trade creates wealth, and that is true whether the trade is interpersonal, interstate, or international. The reality is that labor outsourcing is simply part of a worldwide trend toward increased international trade in both goods and services. As international trade expands—assuming politicians and bureaucrats allow it to expand—the result will be higher rates of growth and higher levels of income, in America and elsewhere. And American workers will enjoy just as much of the fruits of that growth as they always have.

## For Critical Analysis

1. What, if any, differences exist between competition among service workers across the fifty states and competition among service workers across nations?

2. When BMW decides to build a plant in the United States, who gains and who loses?

3. In 2004, International Business Machines Corporation (IBM) stated that it expected to save almost $170 million annually starting in 2006 by shifting several thousand high-paying programming jobs overseas. Explain why IBM would undertake this move. Then explain the short-run and long-run effects of this outsourcing.

# part TWO

# The Business Cycle, Unemployment, and Inflation

# What's in a Word? Plenty, When It's the 'R' Word

Incumbent presidents (and members of their political party) hate the 'R' word. We speak here of **recession,** a word used to describe a downturn or stagnation in overall, nationwide economic activity. Politicians' attitudes toward recessions are driven by the simple fact that, as we note elsewhere, people tend to "vote their pocketbooks." That is, when the economy is doing well, voters are likely to return incumbent politicians to office, but when the economy is doing poorly, voters are likely to "throw the bums out." Interestingly, although *recession* is the word most commonly used to describe a period of poor performance by the economy, most people don't really know what the word means.

## Enter the NBER

Ever since its founding in 1920, a private organization called the National Bureau of Economic Research (NBER) has sought to accurately measure the true state of overall economic conditions in the United States. (It also sponsors a wide variety of research on other economic issues, but those are not our concern here.) Over time, the NBER developed a reputation for measuring the economy's performance in an even-handed and useful way. As a result, most people now accept without argument what the NBER has to say about the state of the economy. And most notably, this means that it is the NBER that we rely on to tell us when we are in a recession.

If you are an avid reader of newspapers, you may well have heard a recession defined as any period in which there are at least two quarters (three-month periods) of declining **real gross domestic product (real GDP).** In fact, the NBER's recession-dating committee places little reliance on the performance of real (inflation-adjusted) GDP when deciding on the state of the economy. There are two reasons for this. First, the government measures GDP only on a quarterly basis, and the NBER prefers to focus on more timely data that are available at least monthly. Second, the official GDP numbers are subject to frequent and often substantial revisions, so what once looked like good economic performance might suddenly look bad, and vice versa. Looking back at 2001 (admittedly a turbulent year), for example, the initial figures showed that real GDP declined in only one quarter during the year. But when the government finally finished all of its revisions to the data, it turned out that real GDP actually fell during *three* quarters of 2001. One can easily see why an organization such as the NBER, which prides itself on reliability and accuracy, might be reluctant to place too much weight on measures of real GDP.

So what *does* the NBER use as its criteria in measuring a recession? Well, the NBER's official definition of a recession gives us some insight:

> A recession is a significant decline in activity spread across the economy, lasting more than a few months, visible in industrial production, employment, real income, and wholesale-retail sales.

Those are a lot of words to define just one term, but it's not too difficult to get a handle on it. The point to note at the outset is that the NBER focuses chiefly on four separate pieces of information:

- Industrial production
- Employment
- Real income (measured by inflation-adjusted personal income of consumers)
- Sales at both the wholesale and the retail levels

All of these figures are reliably available on a monthly basis, and so every month the NBER uses the latest figures on each to take the pulse of the economy. When all four are moving upward, that's generally good news. When all are moving downward, that's definitely bad news. And when some are moving in one direction and some in another direction, that's when expert judgment comes into play.

## The Three *D*'s

If the NBER recession-dating committee uses a strict formula to time the onset or end of a recession, the committee members certainly don't reveal what it is. What they do reveal is that they are looking for three crucial elements—all starting with the letter *D*—when they officially announce the start or end of a recession:

- *Depth*—If there is a downturn in one or more of the key variables listed above, the NBER focuses first on the magnitude of that downturn. For example, in an economy like ours with total employment of 140 million, a drop in employment of 50,000 would not be crucial; an employment drop of, say, one million surely would be considered significant.
- *Duration*—Month-to-month fluctuations in economic activity are the norm in our economy. These fluctuations occur partly because our measures of economic activity are imperfect and partly because, in an economy as complex as ours, many things are happening all the time that have the capacity to affect the overall performance of the economy. Thus, if real personal income moves up or down for a month or even two months in a row, the recession-dating committee is likely to determine that such a change is well within the bounds of normal variation. But if a change persists for, say,

six months, then the committee is likely to place a much heavier weight on that movement.

- *Dispersion*—Because the NBER is trying to measure the overall state of the economy, it wants to make sure it is not being misled by economic developments that, although they may be important to many people, are not reliable indicators of the overall state of the economy. For example, America is becoming less dependent on industrial production and more reliant on service industries. In addition, it is well known that industrial production is sensitive to sharp movements not shared by sectors elsewhere in the economy. Thus, the NBER tempers the importance of industrial production by simultaneously relying on measures such as wholesale and retail sales to make sure it has a picture of what is happening throughout the economy.

## And the Answer Is . . .

Having blended its four measures of the economy together in a way that reflects its focus on the "three *D*'s," the recession-dating committee makes its decision. A recession, in its view, begins "just after the economy reaches a peak of activity" and ends "as the economy reaches its trough" (that is, starts expanding again). Between trough and peak, the economy is said to be in an **expansion.** Historically, the normal state of the economy is expansion; most recessions are brief (usually no more than twelve to eighteen months), and in recent decades they have been rare. Our most recent recession began in March 2001, after exactly ten full years of economic expansion, and ended in November 2001.

The four measures used by the NBER to date recessions generally move fairly closely together. Although they individually sometimes give conflicting signals for short periods of time, they soon enough start playing the same song. Nevertheless, some contention about the NBER's decisions remains. There are two sources of debate. One focuses on *potential* growth of economic activity, while the other highlights the importance of population growth.

The NBER defines a recession as an absolute decline in economic activity. But some economists note that, at least for the last 200 years or so, growth in economic activity from year to year has been the norm in most developed nations, including the United States. Hence, they argue, a recession should be declared whenever growth falls significantly below its long-term potential. This dispute becomes more important when there is reason to believe potential growth has shifted for some reason or when comparing the current performance of two nations that are growing at different rates. For example, suppose nation X has potential growth of 4 percent per year, while nation Y has potential growth of only 2 percent per year. If both are actually growing at 2 percent, the unemployment rate in X will be rising, and some people would argue that this is sufficient to declare that X is in a state of recession. The biggest problem with this proposed measure of recession is that it is difficult to declare with confidence exactly what the potential growth rate of any country is.

The second point of contention starts with the observation that the population is growing in most countries. Hence, even if economic activity is growing, the well-being of the average citizen might not be. For example, suppose the population is growing 3 percent per year but real personal income is growing only 2 percent a year. Assuming the other measures of activity were performing like personal income, the NBER would say the economy was in an expansion phase, even though real per capita income was clearly declining. Some economists would argue that this state of affairs should be declared a recession, given that the term is supposed to indicate a less-than-healthy economy. This point certainly has some validity. Nevertheless, there have not been many prolonged periods when the NBER has said the economy was expanding, and yet per capita income was falling.

Ultimately, of course, even if the recession-dating committee somehow tinkered with its methods to better acknowledge the importance of potential growth and population changes, some *other* issue undoubtedly would be raised to dispute the NBER's conclusions. For now, most economists are content to rely on the NBER to make the call. Most politicians are too—except, of course, when it suits them otherwise. As for the average voter, well, even if she doesn't know how a recession is defined, she surely knows what one feels like—and is likely to vote accordingly.

## For Critical Analysis

1. Why is it important, both for the political process and for our understanding of the economy, for the NBER to resist the temptation to change its definition of a recession to fit the latest political pressures or economic fads?

2. Do you think that voters care more about whether the NBER says the economy is in a state of recession or whether they and their friends and family members are currently employed in good jobs? Why do politicians make a big deal over whether the economy is "officially" in a recession or an expansion? (HINT: Is it hard for the average voter to tell what is going on in the economy outside his or her community, leaving the voter dependent on simple measures—or labels—of what is happening elsewhere in the economy?)

3. Examine the data from the last six recessions. (Good sources for data are http://www.nber.org/cycles/recessions.html and http://www.bea.doc.gov/ and http://www.globalindicators.org.) Rank them on the basis of both duration and severity. The first is easy; the second is more difficult: Is it possible that some people—either politicians or other citizens—might disagree about how to measure the severity of a particular recession? How would you measure it?

# The Case of the
# Disappearing Workers

Every month, the Bureau of Labor Statistics (BLS) goes out into the labor market to determine how many unemployed people there are in the United States. With the data it acquires, the BLS calculates the **unemployment rate.** This number is a key indication of how well the economy is doing. The unemployment rate is calculated in a seemingly straightforward way: it is the percentage of the total **labor force** that is (1) over age 16 but not in institutions or school and (2) actively seeking employment but not found it.

The reelection chances of incumbent presidents often hinge on the estimated rate of unemployment. Historically, when the unemployment rate is rising, the president's chances of reelection have been far worse than when the rate is stable or falling. As the old saying goes, "people vote their pocketbooks" (or, in this case, their pay stubs).

For this and a variety of other reasons, understanding how the unemployment rate is measured is important for politicians and laypeople alike. Remarkably, however, there is little consensus about the accuracy of unemployment statistics in the United States. First, consider the period when the United States had its greatest measured rate of unemployment—the Great Depression, which started in 1929 and did not fully end until the start of World War II.

## 25 Percent Unemployment—Hard to Imagine

If you look at official government statistics on the unemployment rate during the Great Depression, you will find that in some statistical series, the rate hit almost 25 percent—meaning that one in four Americans who were part of the labor force could not find a job during the depths of the Depression. That high unemployment rate, of course, makes any recession since then seem like child's play in terms of the number of people adversely affected.

Some economists, though, are not so sure that approximately one-fourth of the labor force was actually unemployed during the Great Depression. The reason is simple: at that time, the federal government instituted numerous programs to "put people back to work." These included the Works Progress Administration (WPA), the Civilian Conservation Corps (CCC), and various lesser programs. Government statisticians decided that all those who were working in such "make-work" programs for the federal government would have been unemployed without the programs. Consequently, the statisticians decided to count as unemployed the millions of Americans who were working under these government programs. Economist Michael Darby of UCLA subsequently recalculated unemployment statistics for the depths of the Great Depression. After adjusting for people who were actually working but were counted as unemployed, he found a maximum unemployment rate of 17 percent. This number is still the highest we have had in modern times, but it is certainly not one-fourth of the labor force.

How much sense does Darby's adjustment make? The argument against the official government statistics is straightforward— the federal government taxed individuals and businesses to pay for those workers at the WPA and CCC. Had the federal government not taxed individuals and businesses to pay for the new government employees, the private sector would have had more disposable income, more spending, and higher employment.

Whether all of those people would have gotten private-sector jobs remains an unanswered question, but it is equally clear that the official numbers greatly overstate the true unemployment rate during the Great Depression.

## Discouraged Workers—A Cover for a Higher "True" Unemployment Rate?

After they have spent some period of time within the pool of the unemployed, certain individuals may get discouraged about their future job prospects. As a result, they may leave the labor market to go back to school, to retire or return to retirement, to work full-time in their households without any explicit pay, or just to do nothing much. Whichever path they take, when interviewers from the Bureau of Labor Statistics ask these individuals whether they are actively looking for a job, they say "no." Individuals such as these are often referred to as **discouraged workers.** They might seek work if labor market conditions were better and potential wages were higher, but they have decided that such is not the case, so they have left the labor market. For years, some critics of the officially measured unemployment rate have argued that during recessions, the rising numbers of discouraged workers cause the government to grossly underestimate the actual rate of unemployment.

To get a feel for the labor market numbers, let's look at the 1990s—perhaps one of the greatest periods of rising employment in U.S. history. During that decade, the number of Americans who were unemployed fell by over five million. Moreover, far fewer workers settled for part-time jobs. Many who had been retired came back to work, and many of those about to retire continued to work. There were even large numbers of students who left school to take high-paying jobs in the technology sector.

The onset of the 2001 recession produced a turnaround in all of those statistics. The number of unemployed rose by about 2.5 million individuals. The number of part-time workers who indicated that they would like to work full-time rose by over one million. And the proportion of those out of work for more than half a year increased by over 50 percent.

According to some economists, another two million workers dropped out of the labor force—the so-called discouraged worker problem. For example, economist Robert Topel of the University of Chicago claims, "The unemployment rate does not mean what it did twenty years ago." He argues that employment opportunities for the least skilled workers no longer exist in today's labor market, so such individuals have simply left the labor force—discouraged and forgotten by the statisticians who compile the official numbers.

## Not Everyone Is Convinced That Discouraged Workers Are a Problem

Other economists argue differently. They note that the labor market is no different from any other market, so we can examine it using supply and demand analysis just as we do with any other good or service. The **labor supply curve** is upward sloping. That means that as overall wages rise (corrected for inflation, of course), the quantity of labor supplied would be expected to increase. After all, when the inflation-corrected price of just about anything else goes up, we observe that the quantity supplied goes up, too. Therefore, argue these economists, the concept of discouraged workers is basically flawed. They say it makes no more sense to talk of discouraged workers than it would to talk of "discouraged apples" that are no longer offered for sale when the price of apples falls.

Because of the upward-sloping supply curve of labor, when real wages rise economywide, we expect retirees and those just about to retire to return to, or remain in, the labor market. We expect students to quit school early if the wages they can earn are relatively high. The opposite must occur when we go into a recession or the economy stagnates. That is to say, with reduced wage growth (or even declines in economywide real wages) and reduced employment opportunities, we expect more young people to stay in school longer, retirees to stay retired, and those about to retire to actually do so. In other words, we expect the same behavior in response to incentives that we observe in all other markets.

## Disability Insurance and
## Labor Force Participation

It is also worth noting that some, perhaps many, of the departures from the labor force by low-skill individuals may actually be prompted by certain government programs. We refer here to a portion of the Social Security program that has expanded dramatically over the past fifteen years or so. It involves **disability payments.** Originally established in 1956 as a program to help those individuals under age 65 who are truly disabled, Social Security Disability Insurance (SSDI) has become the federal government's fastest-growing program, as the real value of benefits has steadily risen and as the Social Security Administration gradually has made it easier for individuals to meet the legal criteria for being "disabled." It now accounts for about $60 billion in federal spending per year. Under SSDI, even those who are not truly disabled can receive payments from the government when they do not work. In addition, because Social Security also offers Supplemental Security Income (SSI) payments for disabled people who have little or no track record in the labor force, some people are calling disability insurance the centerpiece of a new U.S. welfare state. Just consider that since 1990, the number of people receiving disability payments from the Social Security Administration has more than doubled to over 5.5 million—perhaps not surprising when you consider that the real value of the monthly benefits a person can collect has gone up 50 percent in the last thirty years. The federal government now spends more on disability payments than on food stamps or unemployment benefits.

What does this mean? Simply that those who might have worked through chronic pain and temporary injuries—particularly those without extensive training and education—have chosen to receive a government disability benefit instead. The average Social Security disability payment is $800 a month, tax-free. For many at the lower echelons of the job ladder, $800 a month tax-free seems pretty good. Indeed, those receiving disability payments make up the largest group of the two million or so who left the labor force during the latest recession. And because people respond to incentives, we can be sure of one thing: whatever happens to the economy in the future, if the real value of disability payments keeps rising, so too will the number of people with disabilities.

## For Critical Analysis

1. To what extent do you believe that the existence of unemployment benefits increases the duration of unemployment and consequently the unemployment rate? (HINT: Use demand analysis and opportunity cost.)
2. Is it possible for the unemployment rate to be "too low"? In other words, can you conceive of a situation in which the economy would be worse off in the long run because there is not enough unemployment?
3. It is believed that much of the increase in the number of people collecting SSDI has resulted from decisions by workers at the U.S. Social Security Administration (SSA) to make it easier to qualify for benefits. How are the disability rules set by SSA workers likely to change depending on (i) whether the SSA budget is held constant or expands when the number of SSDI recipients rises; (ii) the overall state of the economy, especially the unemployment rate; and (iii) the likelihood that individuals with disabilities will be discriminated against in the workplace?

# 8

# *The Graying of the Workforce*

America is aging. The baby boomers who pushed the Beatles and the Rolling Stones to stardom during the 1960s and 1970s are racing into middle age. Indeed, the future of America is now on display in Florida, where one person in five is over 65. In 30 years, almost 20 percent of *all* Americans will be 65 or older.

## The Forces behind America's Senior Boom

Two principal forces are behind America's "senior boom." First, we're living longer. Average life expectancy in 1900 was 47. Today, it is over 77, and it is likely to reach 80 within the next decade. Second, the birthrate is low by historical standards. Today's mothers are having far fewer children than their mothers had. In short, the old are living longer, and the ranks of the young are growing too slowly to offset that unmistakable reality. Together, these forces are pushing up the proportion of the population over 65; indeed, the population of seniors is growing at twice the rate of the rest of the population. In 1970, the **median age** in the United States—the age that divides the older half of the population from the younger half—was 28; by 2004, the median age was 37 and rising rapidly.

The aging of America is not just apparent in senior citizen communities, however. It is also showing up in the workforce. According to the 2000 census, there were 61 million Americans aged 45 to 64; by 2010, it is estimated that there will be 79 million in this age bracket. This is a 30 percent jump, much larger than the 11 percent increase that is expected to occur among all people age 16 and above. Thus, roughly one in three working-age Americans will soon be "mature", this being the polite way of saying they'll be 45 or older.

At first blush, all those mature workers might seem to be a serious impediment to career progress on the part of those under 45. In fact, however, plenty of people who once would have kept working until they dropped have instead opted for retirement. In 1960, for example, 78 percent of men aged 60 to 64 were in the workforce, as were 31 percent of those 65 and older. But today, those figures are down to about 55 and 17 percent, respectively. In short, older workers are leaving the workplace in record numbers, yielding an average age at retirement of 62, down from 65 in 1963.

## The Workplace Exodus

Part of the exodus of mature workers is due simply to their prosperity. Older people have higher **disposable incomes** than any other age group in the population and are using that income to consume more leisure. Importantly, however, the changing work habits of older individuals have been prompted—perhaps inadvertently—by three practices of U.S. businesses:

- Career advancement often slows after age 40.
- Over 60 percent of U.S. corporations offer early retirement plans.
- Only about 5 percent offer inducements to delay retirement.

Looking ahead to career dead ends and hefty retirement checks, increasing numbers of older workers are opting for the golf course instead of the morning commute.

Even more important than the policies of businesses, however, may be the federal government's tax treatment of the elderly. Individuals age 65 and over, especially those in middle-income brackets, can be subject to a crushing array of taxes. Among other levies, they must pay taxes on up to 85 percent of their Social Security benefits. And, for those who retire at age 62 and want to work at another job while collecting Social Security, they not only must pay payroll taxes, but they also lose $1 in Social Security benefits for every $2 of wage income over about $12,000. Because these taxes can "piggyback" on each other, effective **marginal tax rates** can become truly astronomical for older workers. In fact, for a fairly typical couple trying to supplement their retirement checks, income from work can be subject to a tax rate up to 80 percent, turning a $10-per-hour part-time job into a $2-per-hour pittance. It's little wonder that so many seniors are saying "no thanks" to seemingly attractive jobs.

Of course, sometimes the jobs say "no thanks" to the mature workers, resulting in unemployment. Overall, the unemployment rate among people age 55 and above is about one-third lower than among the workforce as a whole. That's the good news. But the bad news is that older workers tend to stay unemployed longer; indeed, the **average duration of unemployment** among those 55 and over is about one-third *higher* than it is among the workforce as a whole.

The reason for this pattern of lower but longer unemployment is simple. Younger workers tend to have more general skills and are less certain about where their skills might be put to their best uses. Hence, younger workers tend to move between jobs on a regular basis but have little trouble finding a new job when they leave their old one. Older workers, in contrast, more often have skills that are quite specific to the industry or firm in which they are currently employed. They already know their best employment option and aren't inclined to move around between jobs. But when they do leave work, finding a position that matches well with their precise skills is often difficult and time-consuming. Thus, unemployment that is a nuisance for a younger worker can be a traumatic and financially draining experience for a mature worker.

## The Response of Employers

The narrower, more job-specific skills of mature workers that we noted above tend to make them somewhat less flexible on the job. But this skill blend also has redeeming factors. Mature workers tend to be more loyal to their employers, for example, a factor that can drastically cut recruiting costs. Some firms are beginning to tailor their hiring practices to take advantage of this important difference between younger and older workers.

A major chain of home centers in California, for example, has begun vigorously recruiting senior citizens as sales clerks. The result has been a sharp increase in customer satisfaction. The older workers know the merchandise better and have more experience in dealing with people. Moreover, **turnover** and **absenteeism** have plummeted. People with gray hair, it seems, are immune to "surfer's throat," a malady that strikes younger Californians before sunny weekends.

Other firms have introduced "retirement transition programs." Instead of early retirement at age 55 or 60, for example, older workers are encouraged to cut back on their workweek while staying on the job. Often, such workers get the best of both worlds, collecting a retirement check while working part-time at the same firm. Another strategy recognizes the importance of rewarding superior performance among older workers. At some firms, for example, senior technical managers are relieved of the drudgery of mundane management tasks, and allowed to spend more time focusing on the technical side of their specialties. To sweeten the pot, the package often includes a pay hike.

Apparently, programs such as these are beginning to pay off. In one recent survey, more than 70 percent of the 400 businesses queried gave their older workers top marks for job performance; over 80 percent of the seniors received ratings of excellent or very good for their commitment to quality. And, in addition to the lower training and recruiting costs that come with keeping mature workers on the job, the retention of these workers cuts pension costs sharply. Finally, because older workers are less likely to have school-age children, even health insurance outlays can sometimes be lower when older workers are kept on the job longer.

## Europe Is Even More Mature

As fast as America and its workforce are aging, Europe and its workforce are aging even faster. Indeed, Europe is getting so old that deaths exceed births in more than 40 percent of the regions that make up the **European Union.** And even though immigration is helping to bolster the population and to slow the aging of their workforces, one in every four regions in Europe now has a declining population. The simple fact is that not enough children are being born to replace the current generation.

Unlike America, where some workers are rethinking early retirement, European workers seem increasingly determined to retire as soon as they possibly can. For example, in 1995 the French government wanted to increase the retirement age for certain railroad workers to 55 from 50. Among other things, the government hoped to cut the looming expense of huge pension costs. The response by transport workers was swift and dramatic: a nationwide transportation strike that brought the economy to a standstill for over a month. Eventually, the government backed down.

By the time you read this, retirements will be surging in many industries throughout Europe. Exactly how firms and government agencies will respond to these retirements is still not clear, at least in part because so many employers and politicians seem to be doing their best to avoid thinking about the problem. As one professor of population studies tells his students, Europeans "will only wake up to the problems when they are in their wheelchairs and there is no one there to push them." One hopes that in America we might start thinking a bit sooner than that.

## For Critical Analysis

**1.** How do the payroll taxes levied on the earnings of workers affect their decisions about how much leisure they consume?

2. In general, people who are more productive earn higher incomes and thus pay higher taxes. How would a change in our immigration laws that favored more highly educated and skilled individuals affect today's American college students? Would the admission of better-educated immigrants tend to raise or lower the wages of American college graduates? On balance, would an overhaul of the immigration system benefit or harm today's college students?

3. Analyze how each of the following major policies might affect people's retirement decisions: (i) the provision of government-subsidized health-care benefits to all retirees; (ii) an increase in the real value of Social Security benefits paid to retirees; (iii) a law permitting employers to discriminate against older workers; and (iv) the elimination of advantageous tax treatment of employer-provider health insurance for workers.

# *The Problem with Deflation*

Most of your life, you have probably had to live with rising prices. That is, you have mainly experienced **inflation,** or a rise in the overall price level. Of course, some prices may have fallen, for example, for computers; but overall, you've lived with inflation for a long time.

**Deflation** is a general decline in the level of prices of goods and services. It once was common in our nation's history, but it has not occurred recently. Nonetheless, according to many commentators, during the early 2000s, the United States was at greater risk of deflation than at any time since the 1930s. Why deflation became a possibility in the early years of the twenty-first century and why people might worry about it are two distinct stories.

## The Causes of Deflation

Deflation can arise for either of two reasons. First, it can occur because the nation is growing robustly, due, for example, to rapid population growth or technological progress. This is what was observed in the United States during extended periods between the Civil War and about 1900. New immigrants were flooding into the country, and technological progress, including the spread of railroads and the emergence of the steel, chemical, and other modern industries, was rapidly increasing the output of goods and services. Because the **money supply** in circulation was growing fairly slowly for much of this period, deflation occurred in many years because there simply weren't enough dollars chasing goods to prevent prices in general from falling.

The second source of deflation is restrictive **monetary policy,** especially monetary policy that causes the money supply to shrink. In this case, the resulting decline in the **aggregate demand** for goods and services causes their prices to fall—we get deflation. This is what happened during the early part of the 1930s, the onset of a period that came to be called the Great Depression. During the years 1930 to 1933, the overall price level fell more than 25 percent, the largest four-year deflation in U.S. history. Restrictive monetary policy also contributed some-what to the deflation of the late nineteenth century, but not nearly to the degree observed in the 1930s.

To some extent, people's fears about deflation are colored—and confused—by the experience of the Great Depression. Because restrictive monetary policy was the source of that deflation, falling prices were accompanied by rising unem-ployment. Indeed, as we saw in Chapter 7, unemployment in America and the hardship it brings were greater during the 1930s than before or since. When people think about defla-tion, they tend to think of the Great Depression and forget that it is possible to have deflation without unemployment.

But even when deflation is not accompanied by unemploy-ment, it can be troublesome for the economy, especially when it is not fully anticipated ahead of time. One reason is that most of the debts in a modern society like ours are expressed in terms of dollars. When there is a deflation, the real value, or purchas-ing power, of those dollars goes up. For creditors, this is good news because it means that people now owe them more, meas-ured in terms of goods and services (or so-called *real* terms). But for debtors, this is bad news, and for exactly the same reason.

Deflation raises the real burden of the debts they owe, because they have to pay back the sums owed with dollars that have a higher **purchasing power** than the dollars that were lent to them. If, somehow, the deflation were fully anticipated by everyone, then debtors could negotiate for lower contractual interest rates that would ease their burden during the deflation. But when the deflation is not fully expected—as it typically is not—contractual interest rates do not fall, so that the effective real burden on debtors rises. Although it is possible that deflation's positive effects on creditors and negative effects on debtors could cancel out exactly, often it doesn't happen this way. The result can be significant economic dislocations.

## Some People Are Cash Constrained

Most people base their spending decisions on a long-term view of their income. They don't think just about their immediate, current income. They recognize that they have some **permanent income,** or average sustained level of income, that they can expect to receive and be able to spend over the long run. To take a simple example, if you are normally paid on the first of the month, you typically don't do all of your spending just on payday. Instead, you recognize that you implicitly have an average level of daily income (equal to about one-thirtieth of the paycheck that comes on the first of the month). It is prudent to spend at this average rate throughout the month, even on days when you don't get a paycheck. Moreover, even if you happen to run short of cash between paychecks (perhaps because of unexpected medical expenses), you know you can easily sell some stocks you own, use your credit card more often, or borrow funds from a bank to help bridge the gap.

But some people don't have the luxury of dipping into savings or borrowing when they come up short. Perhaps they are just starting out in the workforce and don't have much of a credit rating or any accumulated savings. More often, they find themselves in this position because they have spent—and borrowed—too much in the past. But either way, they are what we call "cash constrained." That is, a $1 (or $1,000) reduction in their disposable income will immediately lead to an equal reduction in their spending.

People who are cash constrained are often debtors. They may have had to borrow because they faced unexpectedly high expenses (such as medical bills), or because they lost their job or had to cut their working hours. For whatever reason, if there is now a sudden deflation, the real value of their debt obligations goes up, and so, too, does the real value of the debt payments they are required to make each month. This acts just like a reduction in their disposable income, inducing them to cut their spending on goods and services by a corresponding amount. Although the deflation raises the wealth of creditors, they are not cash constrained, so their spending does not rise enough to offset the decline in debtors' spending. The creditors are taking the long view. When the real values of their assets rise in the deflation, they chiefly plan on spending more sometime in the future.

Thus, because of the existence of cash-constrained debtors, the net effect of deflation on the economy can be depressing. The reduced spending caused by the higher burden on debtors is not fully offset by higher spending by the now-richer creditors. Overall, total aggregate demand goes down, and the result can be higher unemployment—and more deflation.

## Bankruptcy Costs Can Be Important

No doubt you've read in the papers that both individuals and businesses sometimes declare **bankruptcy.** For some companies, bankruptcy means going out of business completely, with the result that all or most of the debts they owed to other people are wiped out. For other companies, bankruptcy simply means that the firm arranges to put off paying some or all of its debts until it can get back to profitable operations. For individuals, although they don't "go out of business," bankruptcy does mean that creditors typically lose some or all of the funds owed to them by the individuals.

The relevance of deflation here is that it increases the real value of the indebtedness of many firms and individuals, and this effect is bigger the more indebted they are. Indeed, this effect can be great enough to push some firms or individuals into bankruptcy, if they had not previously anticipated the deflation. Now, although bankruptcy causes losses for creditors, it simultaneously yields some gains for the debtors, because their debts are wiped out. In principle, the creditors' losses could be exactly offset by the debtors' gains, with no net effect on spending in the economy. But, in practice, it doesn't happen this way.

Bankruptcy is extremely costly to society because it uses up or ruins the real value of important assets. Reputations of bankrupt individuals or firms are destroyed. Assets that once were used highly productively by one firm are now dispersed among other firms, where they are not as productive as before. Plus, the time and effort of many people must be devoted to sorting out the mess left by bankruptcy instead of to producing new goods and services.

Overall then, we see that deflation has the potential to increase the incidence of bankruptcy. In so doing, it leads to the emergence of bankruptcy costs—that is, the destruction in asset values that occurs when there is a bankruptcy. Broadly speaking, the wealth of society falls, and the total level of aggregate spending does, too. The result can be a rise in unemployment—and more deflation.

## The Responses to Changing Relative Prices

We usually think of changes in the price level—such as in deflation—as occurring smoothly and evenly. Thus, if deflation is, say, 10 percent per year (as it was from 1932 to 1933), it is natural to think that all prices are moving downward at exactly that same rate of 10 percent per year. If this were true, then the **relative prices** of goods and services would not change during the year, and that would be the end of this part of the story. Unfortunately, things are not this simple.

The fact is that deflation never proceeds evenly and smoothly. No one in 1932 knew that prices were going to fall 10 percent over the next year. Moreover, prices did not fall at exactly the same rate throughout the year. And finally, some prices fell early, while some fell later, so the relative prices of goods changed during the year. All of these developments led people to focus on trying to predict the magnitude and timing of changes in the prices of goods and services, instead of trying to produce new goods and services. The result was that the United States as a society had fewer goods and services available for consumption.

So, we see that there are at least three reasons why we should worry about deflation—that is, the next time deflation actually sets in for any protracted period of time. The fact is that, except for very brief periods, we have had little deflation during the last 70 years in the United States. Instead, as we noted earlier, we have been far more likely to have inflation. But, as we shall see in the next chapter, inflation is also something to be concerned about.

## For Critical Analysis

1. If the deflation during the 1930s had not been accompanied by so much unemployment, would people today be as concerned about deflation as some of them seem to be? Does this suggest that those people are unable to distinguish between the two different sources of deflation? Or does it mean that they think that one of those forces (and not the other) might trigger deflation today?

2. Based on what you have read in the papers and elsewhere, do you think people in the early 2000s thought that deflation was going to occur due to rapidly rising output or to restrictive monetary policy? What evidence can you cite to support your view?

3. How might the effects of deflation differ depending on whether people were surprised by the deflation or they fully expected it ahead of time? For example, how might interest rates differ depending on whether or not the deflation is expected ahead of time? In a world where *inflation* is the norm, how likely is it that if a deflation occurs, people will anticipate it before it happens?

# The Problem with Inflation

> There is no subtler, no surer means of overturning the existing basis
> of society than to debauch the currency. The process engages all the
> hidden forces of economic law on the side of destruction, and does
> it in a manner which not one man in a million is able to diagnose.
> J. M. Keynes, *The Economic Consequences of the Peace,* 1919

What the great economist John Maynard Keynes said more
than eighty years ago remains just as true today. **Inflation**
imposes costs on the economy and exerts stresses on the social
fabric that have the capacity to destroy both. Governments
have been brought to their knees by inflation, and dictators
have been empowered by it. And, although high inflation
might seem a remote possibility for the United States today, it
is a crushing problem in other countries and could easily
return to haunt us in the future.

## The Money Tax

Inflation is a sustained rise in the average price of all goods and
services. It is caused by growth in the **money supply** that exceeds
the rate at which the economy can increase the output of goods
and services. Most often, this occurs because the government
has chosen to issue more money, typically as a means of helping
it finance its activities.

Inflation acts as a tax on people's holdings of money—that
is, their holdings of **currency** and **checkable deposits.** All of
us hold some currency and checkable deposits because of the

convenience they provide. As a result, each of us loses wealth whenever there is inflation, because the **purchasing power** of our money balances falls at the rate of inflation.

Assume, for example, that you have $10 stashed in a compartment of your wallet, in case you need to grab a taxi or a sandwich at the corner deli at 2 A.M. some morning. If after one year there has been a 10 percent rise in the **price level,** then the purchasing power of that piece of paper that says "ten dollars" will be only $9, measured in terms of taxi rides or sandwiches. You will have lost value equal to 10 percent times the amount of currency you kept on hand. (If you were holding checkable deposits over this period, their value would also have fallen, although perhaps by not quite so much, for reasons we'll see below.)

In essence, then, the purchasing power, or real value, of the money we hold depreciates when there is inflation. The only way we can avoid this type of **inflation tax** on the money we hold is to reduce our holdings of money. But doing this is not easy. It is beneficial—productive—to have money on hand to pay for the things that we want when we want them, rather than trying to purchase everything at the beginning of a pay period so as to minimize the dollars in our checkable accounts or in our wallets.

Thus, a cost to society of inflation is that it increases the cost of holding money. Society as a whole, therefore, uses *too little* money during periods of inflation. This effect is greatest for currency, because its real value falls one-for-one with each rise in the price level. But checkable deposits are also affected. Many of these accounts pay some interest, and that nominal interest rate rises when the expected inflation rate rises. This helps reduce the inflation tax on checkable deposits. But **depository institutions** typically do not receive interest on the **reserves** they hold against their deposits. As a result, they are unable to fully compensate depositors for higher inflation. That is, when the inflation rate goes up, the interest rate on checkable deposits rises by a lesser amount, so it becomes more costly to hold these accounts.

Recently, the sum of currency plus the reserves of depository institutions has been about $800 billion, roughly 90 percent of it in currency and the rest in reserves. All of these funds are subject to the full brunt of the inflation tax. Thus, our hypothetical inflation rate of 10 percent would impose a tax of $80 billion per year on people who use money, with about 90 percent of the tax falling on users of currency and the rest landing on users of checkable deposits. Lately, the inflation rate in the United States has been well below 10 percent, but it was *above* 10 percent as recently as the early 1980s. Moreover, even at a 2 percent inflation rate, the users of money still pay a tax of about $16 billion per year. This is enough to induce some users to conserve on money and devote time and effort to finding ways of avoiding the inflation tax on money. All of these efforts could have been used to produce consumable goods and services, so the value of such goods and services is lost to us as a result of inflation.

## The Investment Tax

Because of the rules of our federal and state tax systems, inflation also acts as a tax on the way both individuals and companies do business. As a result, it distorts certain business practices and thus leads to a reduction in our wealth. Let's see how.

Increases in the market value of any **asset** are subject to **capital gains** tax, which is collected when the asset is sold. Suppose you buy an asset for $1,000. This asset might be shares of stock in a corporation or a painting that you hope to sell sometime later for a profit. Now suppose that, several years later, solely because the prices of all goods have gone up by 50 percent, you are able to sell the asset for $1,500. If there were no taxes on capital gains, your wealth would have remained unchanged as a result of this transaction; the asset rose in dollar value by 50 percent, but the purchasing power of those dollars fell correspondingly, so the real value of that asset (and thus your wealth) remained unchanged.

But, in fact, you purchased this asset in the hopes of making a profit, so there are taxes to be paid on the $500 "gain" in the value of the asset. At recent rates, these taxes will amount to about $100 at the federal level and varying additional amounts at the state level. Thus, even though the prices of all goods have risen 50 percent, the *after-tax* value of your investment has risen far less. What seemed to be a gain, in fact, turns out to be a *reduction* in your wealth. You end up poorer than when you began. Had there been no inflation, your later sale of that asset would have taken place at $1,000, and you would not have faced any taxes because you would simply have broken even on the deal.

As a first approximation, then, every time the price level rises, the value of your assets subject to the capital gains tax falls by the proportionate rise in the price level, multiplied by the tax rate. So, a 10 percent rise in the price level, combined with a 20 percent long-term capital gains tax rate, reduces the real value of these assets by 2 percent. This may not sound like much, but it is enough to distort the choices people make, and so it results in lower wealth for us as a society.

Similar problems arise in the course of everyday business transactions. When businesses invest in machines and buildings, for example, they are allowed to deduct as a cost only a certain amount of depreciation each year. For example, if a machine costs $1 million and is supposed to last ten years, under the simplest system of depreciation deductions, the firm can deduct $100,000 a year for ten years from its income before it pays federal corporate profits taxes.

In a world of inflation, however, the old dollar value (the **historical cost**) of a business's investments fails to reflect the **replacement value** of the asset that is being depreciated. Under current federal income tax laws, the replacement value of the asset (what it costs today) cannot be properly adjusted upward to reflect more accurately the higher dollar cost of replacing the depreciating equipment. The result is an over-statement of the true profits (revenues minus total cost) earned by the firm. This overstatement leads to the payment of higher federal corporate taxes. This, in turn, reduces businesses' incentive to invest in these productive assets and so reduces our wealth, now and in the future.

## The Exchange Tax

We usually think of the price level as changing smoothly and evenly. In fact, inflation never proceeds evenly and smoothly; a positive inflation rate is almost always an *uncertain* and *uneven* inflation rate, which leads people into all sorts of costly behavior.

When inflation is positive, more resources are devoted to predicting the rate of inflation and to avoiding the effects of inflation. Individuals attempt to negotiate **escalator clauses** (calling for automatic wage increases when the price level rises) into their contracts, a procedure that requires time and effort as well as legal and accounting resources. New institutions arise to accommodate markets in a world of variable, uncertain rates of inflation. During the late 1970s and early 1980s, for example, a new type of home mortgage contract seemed to appear every year to take account of wildly changing rates of inflation. Moreover, when people are relying more on escalator, or cost-of-living, clauses in contracts, more resources will be devoted to measuring price changes more accurately.

The uneven character of inflation means that the **relative prices** of goods change more often and by larger amounts than when the overall price level is stable. Consumers choose on the basis of relative prices. Even when inflation is variable and uncertain, consumers have little difficulty determining the relative prices of frequently purchased goods, such as food, because they regularly observe prices of these goods. During inflationary times, however, a consumer who enters the marketplace seeking a less frequently purchased item, such as a major appliance or a car, often is shocked at how high the prices are. To obtain further information about prices, the consumer feels compelled to search longer than would be the case in a world without inflation. Ultimately, the consumer often will still buy the item but only after spending considerable resources in time and comparison shopping efforts.

Matters are even worse when inflation really heats up. In countries such as Brazil, where the annual inflation rate in some years has run at 200 percent or more, it may even pay to shop around for regularly purchased items, such as food and clothing, because of the uneven pace at which prices change. The prices of some goods change monthly; for others, prices adjust daily. Some shops hike their prices early in the week; others late in the week. Thus, the *relative* prices of identical items sold at two different times or places can vary markedly—20 percent or more—over short periods of time. Clearly, shoppers have a strong incentive to make sure they are buying goods that have the "oldest" prices, and many do just that—they spend many hours each week making sure they don't buy items whose prices have just gone up. And, of course, all of this time and effort spent searching for better prices could have been spent producing goods and services. It is rational for people to engage in the inflation-induced search—but it is also costly for them and for society as a whole.

## The Work Tax

About thirty-five years ago the inflation rate in the United States heated up, so Congress decided to put an escalator clause into the Social Security system. In particular, Social Security benefits were tied, or indexed, to the **consumer price index (CPI)**, changes in which provide one measure of the inflation rate. The idea was to ensure that the real value of retirees' benefits would not be reduced by inflation. In fact, the indexing of benefits turned out to cause the real value of these benefits to *rise*.

The CPI tends to overstate the true rate of inflation because it fails to adequately account for the rising quality and selection of goods over time, and it also fails to adjust for the ability of people to switch between goods when the price of one rises relative to another. The magnitude of this overstatement depends on a variety of factors, but the best estimate is that the CPI overstated the inflation rate, on average, by around 1.1 percentage points per year over much of the last thirty-five years. Thus, every time the price level rose, the *real* value of Social Security benefits rose. Recent revisions to the method of computing the CPI have cut the bias to perhaps 0.8 percent per year, but the remaining bias continues to push up the real value of Social Security benefits year after year. Overall, indexing benefits to the CPI has caused the real value of the benefits to rise by over 40 percent.

Here, as elsewhere, people respond to incentives. The rising value of Social Security benefits makes the opportunity cost of working higher for people when they reach the age of benefit eligibility. Thus, some of them retire earlier than they would have in the absence of this increase in real Social Security benefits. This, in turn, reduces the amount of goods and services produced by the economy. Again, the magnitude of this effect, like the other effects we have been talking about, is probably modest—as long as the inflation rate stays modest. But if we forget about these effects, chances are that inflation won't remain modest. Moreover, the cumulative consequences of a large number of modest effects can be large. As the late U.S. Senator Everett Dirksen once said, "A million here and a million there, and pretty soon you're talking real money." This is as true now as it was over eighty years ago, when John Maynard Keynes worried about the problem with inflation.

## For Critical Analysis

1. If inflation is so costly, why do you suppose it is so commonplace in modern societies?
2. In light of your answer to the preceding question, what keeps governments from escalating inflation rates ever higher and higher?
3. During the 1990s, the federal government reduced the average maturity of its debt obligations, replacing longer maturity debts with shorter maturity debts. (The maturity of a debt is the length of time between when the money is borrowed and when the amount must be paid back.) What has this change in the average maturity of the government's debt done to its incentive to engage in inflationary policy? (Hint: Typically, when federal debt comes due, the government simply borrows more funds to pay off the old debt—and it must borrow at whatever interest rates are then prevalent.)

# 11

# The Futility of
# Price Controls

In the modern world, **inflation** seems to be just about everywhere. Among the 167 nations for which data are available, 164 (that's 98.2 percent) experienced sustained inflation throughout the 1990s. Sixteen of these countries, including Brazil and Russia, had inflation rates that averaged more than 100 percent *per year* during this period. Although it looks like the first decade of the twenty-first century will have fewer members of the "100 percent club," almost every nation will once again have another decade of sustained inflation.

Over the sweep of history, inflation has been less commonplace than today, but it is most assuredly not a modern phenomenon. The ancient Greek philosopher Aristotle was aware of inflation, and long before the birth of Christ, ancient Rome was plagued by rising prices. We now know that sustained inflation is, in the words the Nobel Laureate Milton Friedman, "everywhere and always a monetary phenomenon." That is, sustained inflation in the long run is the result of growth in the **money supply** that exceeds the rate at which the economy can increase the output of goods and services. This means that the cure for inflation is simple: reduce the rate at which the money supply is growing.

This cure for inflation has rarely been popular with governments, however, because they routinely have been the *source* of rapid growth in the money supply. (In fact, issuing more and more money is one of the more popular means by which governments finance their activities, particularly during wars and other periods of fiscal stress.) Instead, governments often have tried to control inflation by imposing legally mandated controls on prices. Despite the popularity of these controls, the evidence is clear: they do not achieve their supposed objective of reducing the true inflation rate, but they have plenty of other consequences, none of them productive.

## The Sweep of History

Although the Egyptians and Babylonians had tried them hundreds of years before, the first well-documented system of price controls was instituted in 301 C.E. by the Roman emperor Diocletian. His price-control edicts set schedules for 890 different price categories, more than 200 of which covered food items. Anyone caught disobeying the emperor's edict was dealt with severely—death by drowning. According to the historian Lactantius, writing in 314, there was

> much bloodshed upon very slight and trifling accounts; and the people brought provisions no more to market since they could not get a reasonable price for them, and this increased the dearth so much that after many had died by it, the law itself was laid aside.

Price controls were resurrected in medieval Europe, with a "just price" code based on the "intrinsic value" of goods. Some years later, the New World colonies tried their hand at controls. In 1636, the Puritans decreed that those who violated wage and price limitations were officially classified with "adulterers and whoremongers."

The high inflation experienced during the American Revolution led eventually to the imposition of price controls. The Continental Congress decreed "that all manufactures of this country be sold at reasonable prices" and that "vendors of goods or merchandise will not take advantage of the scarcity of goods, . . . but will sell the same at rates we have been respectively accustomed to for twelve months last past." But such admonitions—supplemented by price controls imposed by most of the colonies—did not prevent inflation. By November of 1777, commodity prices were 480 percent above their pre-war average expressed in terms of paper money, or "continentals."

The controls did, however, cause sometimes serious disruptions in the supplies of goods and services. General George Washington had great difficulty acquiring army provisions at controlled prices, a problem that played a key role in the agony his troops endured at Valley Forge during the winter of 1777–1778. Partly as a result, the Continental Congress urged the states to abolish controls, declaring in June 1778 that "It hath been found by Experience that Limitations upon the Price of Commodities are not only ineffectual for the Purposes proposed, but are likewise productive of very evil Consequences to the great Detriment of the Public Service and grievous Oppression of Individuals."

Nonetheless, many local and state price controls continued. At some town meetings, the names of those who charged more than the controlled prices were announced, and the guilty were condemned in newspapers. Boston declared that those who violated price ceilings were enemies of their country. By 1780, most controls were abandoned.

America's most comprehensive attempt at controlling prices occurred during World War II. Some years later, in the 1970s the Nixon administration instituted extensive wage and price controls, during the Vietnam War. And throughout the country, state and local governments have tried to control the prices of a variety of individual goods. For example, many states have laws prohibiting "price gouging" (usually invoked to control the price of gasoline or ice for refrigeration after natural disasters, such as major storms or earthquakes), and dozens of cities have controls on the rents that landlords may charge on apartments.

## Why Impose Controls?

The most popular justification for imposing wage and price controls at the national level focuses on the importance of expectations. The claim is that, either as a result of past inflation or in expectation of future inflation, firms raise prices. These price increases lead other firms to expect more inflation, which leads them to raise prices, and so forth. Imposing price controls, it is said, will break the "expectations cycle" and thus stop the upward pressure on prices.

Although this is a plausible argument, it glosses over the fundamental *source* of inflation. After all, inflation is a generalized increase in the dollar prices of goods and services. For it to occur, something must change the money supply (or the demand for money) relative to the supply of goods and services. Looking at the historical record, the source of such change almost always has been excessive monetary growth. Moreover, this excessive monetary growth almost always has been caused by government issuance of money to finance its expenditures.

But why impose controls rather than going after the root of the problem? When price controls are imposed at the national level, there are a few possible explanations. During wartime, the government necessarily reallocates huge amounts of resources from private consumption to the war effort. Price controls can help promote patriotic unity by spreading the cost of that reallocation more evenly among people than if prices freely adjusted and **wealth** or **income** alone determined **consumption.** Then, too, the controls sharply reduce the budgetary cost of the resource requirements of the war, making the full cost less obvious and thus politically more palatable. (Note that price controls do *not* reduce the real economic cost of the war; in fact, they increase it because they force people to use more costly, nonprice means of allocating scarce resources, such as standing in line.) The imposition of peace-time price controls by a national government is most often an attempt to distract voters' attention from the real source of the inflation—namely, government spending far in excess of its political will or ability to levy explicit taxes.

State and local governments have no power to issue money, so they cannot cause—or stop—inflation. But these governments do have both the power and the inclination to reallocate resources among their citizens. Price controls are one way to accomplish this. For example, legal ceilings on the prices (rental rates) that landlords may charge on apartments reallocate wealth from landlords (who are few in number) to tenants (who are numerous). This often yields votes for the politicians imposing these controls.

## The Consequences of Controls

Price controls of the type we are discussing reduce actual prices below their equilibrium levels. This implies that price controls must necessarily have three consequences:

- The lower prices received by suppliers induce them to reduce the quantities of the goods supplied on the market.
- The reductions in the quantities of the goods supplied must raise the *full* cost of the goods to consumers, including both price and nonprice costs (such as waiting in line).
- Because scarce goods can no longer be rationed by prices, some nonprice means of **rationing** must arise, such as a decline in the quality of goods supplied or the emergence of lengthy waits in line for the privilege of purchasing at the controlled price.

We noted earlier that the price controls imposed by Diocletian led to reduced supplies of goods and the emergence of bloodshed as a rationing device. Similarly, the price controls imposed by Pennsylvania during the American Revolution made it impossible for General Washington to properly feed and clothe his troops at Valley Forge. And only a few years later, when the French Revolutionary government felt compelled to institute price controls, the effects were immediate. As one commentator noted: "The butcher in weighing meats added more scraps than before . . . other shopkeepers sold second-rate goods at the maximum [price] . . . . The common people complained that they were buying pear juice for wine, the oil of poppies for olive oil, ashes for pepper, and starch for sugar."

Of course, governments try to prevent people from responding in these ways. Yet policing the controls on millions of prices is an enormous task. During World War II, the United States had approximately 60,000 paid price watchers and 300,000 to 350,000 volunteer price watchers. The time and effort devoted to policing price controls use **economic resources** that are, by definition, not free. And even so, no system of policing can be complete. As one later administrator of U.S. price controls put it, "No matter how cleverly any group designs a control system, distortions and inequities will appear."

The truth in this statement is illustrated by government attempts to control gasoline prices in the United States during the 1970s. In 1973, several major Arab oil-producing nations refused to ship oil to the United States and other Western nations, in retaliation for Israel's so-called Yom Kippur War with Egypt and Syria. The result was a significant reduction in world oil supplies and sharp upward pressure on gasoline prices. Again in 1979, oil-producing states, acting in concert through the Organization of Petroleum Exporting Countries (OPEC), decided to cut world oil supplies—which once more put strong upward pressure on gasoline prices. The U.S. government tried to resist these pressures with price controls on gasoline—and the results were disastrous.

Faced with soaring input costs and unable to pass these costs on to consumers, gas-station owners sharply reduced their hours and limited the amount of gasoline that customers could buy at one time. As consumers frantically sought fuel, lengthy lines formed at gas stations. Some lines reportedly stretched a mile or more, and people often had to wait hours for the opportunity to buy five or ten gallons of gasoline.

Some station owners tried to alleviate the problem by offering to fill up the customer's gas tank before the station's regular opening hours, *if* the customer would park in the station lot the night before—for a minor "parking fee" of, say, $25. Drivers tried to help, too, by offering to buy one-gallon gas cans at four times their regular price—if they were full of gas. But such behavior was deemed illegal by the government, and so the gas lines continued. Not surprisingly, tempers began to flare. One man who cut in line ahead of other people was beaten senseless by another driver wielding a metal tire iron. Another driver who jumped to the head of a gas line pulled a gun when informed by the attendant that he would have to return to his assigned spot. Reportedly, he got his gas—and was later arrested. Interestingly, in Europe and Japan, where prices were generally allowed to rise in response to the reduced supplies, there were no lines, no special parking deals, and no reports of gas-station violence.

## Do They Work?

The *measured* rate of inflation during World War II was certainly lower with price controls than it would have been without them. But what do we mean by the rate of inflation? If we mean the rate of increase in the consumer price index (CPI), that measure may have little to do with the *actual* rate of inflation. During World War II, the CPI rose very little because in most cases any explicit, published rise in prices was illegal! We had then what has been called a **repressed inflation:** inflation was actually going on, but it did not show up in the official, published price indices. People had to resort to a variety of costly devices to obtain goods at the official, controlled prices; this drove the full cost of goods well above the level indicated by published prices. When price controls were lifted after the war, the official price index caught up with the actual price index, and, for two or three years, published prices rose very rapidly.

This brings up one of the more peculiar aspects of price controls: the more effective they *seem* to be, the more likely they are to be *ineffective*. We have already seen how price controls lead to declines in product quality and to costly alternative means of rationing the goods. But in addition, sometimes the supplies of the goods disappear altogether. What does a price index mean when, during periods of price controls, many goods are not even available? In fact, the true price of many items during periods of controls is actually *infinite* because they are unavailable. What happens to the true cost of goods when the price of even one item goes to infinity? Surely, General Washington's troops must have pondered this question when they found themselves starving at Valley Forge in the winter of 1777–1778.

## For Critical Analysis

1. What happens to the average true cost of all goods when the price of one good goes to infinity?
2. What effect does a maximum price have when the market price is *less* than the maximum legal price?
3. Suppose the equilibrium price of gasoline is $2.00 per gallon and that at this price, the average person purchases ten gallons on each visit to the gas station. Now assume that the maximum lawful price for gasoline is set by the government at $1.50 per gallon. At this ceiling price, there will be an excess demand for gasoline. Assume that this excess demand is rationed by waiting in line. If the typical person has to stand in line for an hour to purchase ten gallons of gas, and if that person's time is worth $10 per hour, what is the *full* or *effective* price per gallon of gasoline in the presence of price controls?

# part
# THREE

## Fiscal Policy

# The Return of
# Big Government

In 1996, the forty-second president of the United States, Bill Clinton, declared, "The era of big government is over." Whatever else President Clinton may have been, he was not a prophet. Shortly after he made this declaration, **discretionary spending** by the federal government accelerated at a torrid pace.

## Discretionary versus
## Nondiscretionary Government Spending

Spending by the federal government, and some state governments, can be divided into two types: discretionary and nondiscretionary. Discretionary spending is anything that Congress decides to spend for which it has to appropriate monies in its **appropriation bills** each **fiscal year.** A good example of discretionary spending is the $30 billion spent to help New York City and various private firms that suffered greatly from the terrorist attacks on September 11, 2001. Nondiscretionary spending usually is driven by **entitlement programs.** These are *formula-driven* expenditures. The best examples are Social Security and Medicare, which provide specific formulas, or rules, that automatically decide (1) who is eligible and (2) the amount for which they are eligible. Once the law is passed that dictates how much retired individuals shall receive—that is, the amount to which they are entitled—Congress no longer controls the amount of funds spent on these programs. The only way such nondiscretionary spending can be slowed down or speeded up is if Congress changes the formulas that dictate who gets what and how much they get.

When Bill Clinton confidently uttered his nonprophecy, discretionary spending had actually fallen from 1994 through part of 1995. It was hovering around $550 billion per year. But by 2003 such spending had reached $800 billion a year—so much for the end of big government!

## But Isn't It All Due to September 11?

One can reasonably (but misleadingly) argue that since September 11, 2001, the federal government and state and local governments, too, have had to spend more on antiterrorism measures. Though this statement is true in one sense, the overall government-spending picture, particularly at the federal level, is quite different. Since late 1995, six years before the terrorist attacks, total federal discretionary spending had already been rising rapidly. Admittedly, this spending was eventually supplemented by funds that were voted for spending on homeland security and national defense. But these sums were a small blip on the radar screen of total increases in federal discretionary spending. Roughly $30 billion was spent on homeland security and national defense programs in the months following September 11. Of this amount, $10 billion went to fighting in Afghanistan and about $20 billion to improving transportation security and rebuilding New York City. But in fiscal year 2002, Congress voted an additional $90 billion of new discretionary spending, which included funds for medical research and highway construction. Fiscal years 2003, 2004, and 2005 all witnessed further additions to discretionary federal spending.

What has been true, and will continue to be true into the foreseeable future, is that numerous expenditures that have absolutely *nothing* to do with countering terrorism will be approved in the name of the fight against terrorism. Consider the latest set of "gifts" to the farming sector, one of the most brazen examples of how old-fashioned special interest subsidies can be hidden under the cover of the war on terrorism. Since 1978, farmers have received subsidies of over $300 billion from the federal government, an amount representing almost 10 percent of the nation's *total* net public debt that we have accumulated from all sources over all time. In recognition of the huge amount of spending going to this tiny special interest group, Congress in 1996 passed the Freedom to Farm bill, which was intended to *phase out* subsidies to farmers gradually. Yet not only have the subsidies *increased* since then, but members of Congress from farm states have also used the war on terrorism as a pretext to ask for even more. How have they done this? By including the word *security* in the title of the farm bill to link the "insecurity" that farmers are currently feeling about their future incomes to the insecurity that Americans in general are feeling in the wake of the terrorist attacks.

The latest legislation is the Farm Security Act of 2002. By 2012, the new subsidies added by this law, when combined with existing federal subsidies, will cost U.S. taxpayers about $180 billion. The Farm Security and Rural Investment Act, its full title, was the largest agricultural subsidy in the history of the United States—all in the name of increased "security," of course.

Some observers believe that all manner of spending that is packaged under the banner of homeland security will become a permanent addition to our federal spending apparatus. The federal government will, as a consequence, keep getting larger, not smaller.

## The New Department of Homeland Security

When President George W. Bush proposed the new Department of Homeland Security (DHS), he argued that it would *not* make government larger. Almost everyone now thinks that President

Bush will turn out to be no better as a prophet than his predecessor. In principle, the DHS has simply combined twenty-two
agencies and 170,000 workers to create a more efficient way to
protect Americans at home. Realize, though, that this department is the most massive new bureaucracy since the Department
of Defense (DOD) was created in 1947. The likelihood of the
DHS remaining even close to its original size is small, if not zero.

First, many DHS activities, like DOD activities, are secret. This
reduces the chances that spending on them will be carefully
scrutinized. Second, DHS and DOD activities are supposed to
protect us from people who would do us harm. If a member of
Congress stops a project on budget grounds and an unfortunate
security breach later occurs as a result, that could be the end of
a political career. Finally, DHS activities, like DOD activities, are
complex and far-reaching. It is easy to claim—and difficult to
refute—that a loss of spending on one project will have spillover
effects that will irreparably damage many other projects.

The result with the DOD is a budget that seems immune to
shrinkage. And, of course, plenty of private-sector firms have
an incentive to keep that budget big because they are doing
business with the department. Hence, they lobby for additional
funding so that they, too, can get some of those extra federal
dollars. It is likely that these same incentives will work their
magic with the new DHS budget. Indeed, within a few months
after the DHS asked private corporations to propose new technologies to fight terrorism, some 1,500 companies had pitched
their ideas. Consider one proposal from an enterprising company: Fit every commercial airline seat with metal straps. Why?
To snare potential hijackers. Yet another proposal: Teach tran-
scendental meditation to our enemies. Why? Obviously, to
calm them down. The list, one imagines, is growing.

## The Impact of Social Security and
## Medicare Spending on the Federal Budget

So far, we have discussed mainly federal discretionary spending.
On the horizon, however, looms a serious and growing problem
with two of the most important entitlement programs—Social

Security and Medicare. At the beginning of the twenty-first century, actual outlays for Social Security and Medicare were about 6.5 percent of the nation's annual national income, or, as it is commonly called, **gross domestic product (GDP).** By 2010, that proportion will have risen to 7 percent; by 2025, to 10 percent; and by 2040, to over 12 percent. This increase in spending on these two entitlement programs is due not only to the increased number of retirees from the Baby Boomer generation (those born right after World War II), but also to the aging of the population as a whole, which is projected to continue for the next half-century at least. By 2075, life expectancy at age 65 will have increased by 20 to 25 percent.

The implied burden of this aging and the growing programs is enormous. At the beginning of the twenty-first century, there were 4.3 workers for every person age 65 or over. By 2020, there will be 2.6 workers; by 2050, there will be 2.4; and by 2075, only 2.2. In other words, a working couple will have to provide almost all of the Social Security and Medicare support for a retired person—in addition to supporting themselves and their children. Put somewhat differently, if you think a big piece of your paycheck is going for taxes now, a much larger piece will be departing in the future.

## The True Size of Government

Government at any level does not exist independently of those who live, work, spend, and pay taxes in our society. As an economy, we face a **budget constraint.** Whatever is spent by government—federal, state, and local—is not and cannot be spent by individuals in the nation. Fundamentally, when we talk about the "size" of government, we are talking about the proportion, or percentage, of GDP that government commands. Whatever government commands in terms of spending decisions, private individuals do not command. From this perspective (and this is simple arithmetic), federal, state, and local governments command about 40 percent of GDP. In addition, some observers have argued that the various levels of government also compel businesses and individuals to spend an additional 10 percent of total income to comply with government regulations and **mandates.** If we follow this line of reasoning, the implication is that, directly or indirectly, government in the United States controls the allocation of about one-half of all resources—which leaves only the other half for you.

## For Critical Analysis

1. The Tax Foundation estimates that the direct tax burden of government actually dropped significantly between 2000 and 2004, chiefly due to federal tax cuts in 2003. Based on what you have read above, do you believe that this decline will continue in the future? Why or why not?
2. Why do you think governments in general, not only in the United States, have a tendency to grow, expressed as a percentage of total GDP?
3. Although federal taxes were cut twice between 2001 and 2005, federal spending rose over that span, so the amount of debt owed by the federal government increased. What does this higher level of debt imply about the likely tax burden of the federal government in the future?

# The Myths of Social Security

You have probably heard politicians debate the need to reform Social Security. If you are under the age of 30, this debate has been going on for your entire lifetime. Why has nothing been done? The reason is that the politicians are debating over "facts" that are not facts: most of the claims made about Social Security are myths—urban legends, if you like. Sadly, the politicians have been repeating these myths so often for so long that they believe the myths, and so do their constituents (perhaps, including you). As long as these myths persist, nothing meaningful will be done about Social Security, and the problem will simply get worse. So let's see if we can't cut through the fog by examining some of the worst Social Security myths.

## Myth 1: The Elderly Are Poor

The Social Security program was founded in 1937, as the United States was coming out of the Great Depression. The **unemployment rate** at the time was the highest in our nation's history. Bank runs and the stock market crash of 1929 had wiped out the savings of millions of people. Many elderly people had little or no resources to draw upon in retirement, and their extended families often had few resources with which to help them. In the midst of these conditions, Social Security was established to make sure that the elderly had access to some *minimum* level of income when they retired. It was never meant to be the sole source of retirement funds for senior citizens.

Given the circumstances of the program's founding, it is not surprising that many people associate Social Security with poverty among the elderly. The fact is that both the Social Security program and the financial condition of older people have changed dramatically over the past seventy years. For example, measured in today's dollars, initial Social Security payments were as little as $105 per month and reached a maximum of $436 per month, or about $5,000 per year. Today, however, many recipients are eligible for payments in excess of $20,000 per year. More importantly, people over age 65 are no longer among the poorest in our society.

As a result of many years of a strong economy and their own savings habits, today's elderly have accumulated literally *trillions* of dollars in **assets.** These assets include homes that are fully paid for and substantial portfolios of stocks and bonds. In addition, millions of older Americans are drawing *private* pensions, built up over years of employment. Social Security payments, for example, now provide only about 40 percent of the income of the average retired person, with the rest coming about equally from private pensions, employment earnings, and investment income. Thus, far from being the age group with the highest poverty rate, the elderly actually suffer about 25 percent *less* poverty than the average of all U.S. residents. To be sure, Social Security helps make this possible, but just as surely, only about 10 percent of the elderly are living in poverty. In contrast, the poverty rate among children is twice as high as it is among people over 65.

## Myth 2: Social Security Is Fixed Income

Most economic and political commentators and laypersons alike treat Social Security benefits as a source of fixed income for the elderly, one that supposedly falls in **real purchasing power** as the general **price level** rises. This myth, too, has its roots in the early days of Social Security, when payments were indeed fixed in dollar terms and thus were subject to the ravages of inflation. But this is no longer true. More than thirty years ago, Congress decided to *index* (or link) Social Security payments to a measure of the overall price level in the economy. The avowed reason for this change was to protect Social Security payments from any decline in real value during inflation. In fact, because of the price level measure chosen by Congress, the real value of payments actually *rises* when there is inflation.

Although there are many potential measures of the average price of goods and services, Congress decided to tie Social Security payments to the **consumer price index (CPI)**. The CPI is supposed to measure changes in the dollar cost of consuming a bundle of goods and services that is representative for the typical consumer. Thus, a 10 percent rise in the CPI is supposed to mean that the **cost of living** has gone up by 10 percent. Accordingly, the law provides that Social Security benefits automatically are increased by 10 percent.

As it turns out, however, the CPI actually overstates the true inflation rate: the CPI is said to be *biased upward* as a measure of inflation. This bias has several sources. For example, when the price of a good rises relative to other prices, people usually consume less of it, enabling them to avoid some of the added cost of the good. But the CPI does not take this into account. Similarly, although the average quality of goods and services generally rises over time, the CPI does not adequately account for this fact. Overall, it has been estimated that until recently, the upward bias in the CPI amounted to about 1.1 percentage points per year on average. Revisions to the CPI have reduced this bias to about 0.8 percent per year. Thus, currently, if the CPI says prices have gone up, say, 1.8 percent, they've really gone up only 1.0 percent. Nevertheless, Social Security payments automatically are increased by the full 1.8 percent.

Now, 0.8 or 1.1 percentage points don't sound like much. And if it happened only once or twice, there wouldn't be much of a problem. But almost every year for the last thirty years, this extra amount has been added to benefits. And over a long time, even the small upward bias begins to amount to a real change in purchasing power. Indeed, this provision of the Social Security system has had the cumulative effect of raising real (inflation-adjusted) Social Security benefits by over 40 percent over this period. So, despite the myth that Social Security is fixed income, in reality the benefits grow even faster than inflation.

## Myth 3: There Is a Social Security Trust Fund

For the first few years of Social Security's existence, taxes were collected but no benefits were paid. The funds collected were used to purchase U.S. Treasury bonds, and that accumulation of bonds was called the Social Security Trust Fund. Even today, tax collections (called payroll taxes—see Chapter 14) exceed benefits paid each year—currently by more than $100 billion per year—so that the trust fund now has well over $1 *trillion* in Treasury bonds on its books. Eventually, after the fund reaches a peak of around $2.6 trillion, retiring baby boomers will drive outgoing benefits above incoming tax collections. The bonds will be sold to finance the difference; by around 2030 all of them will be sold, and thereafter all benefits in excess of payroll taxes will have to be financed explicitly out of current taxes.

The standard story told (by politicians, at least) is that the bonds in the trust fund represent net assets, much like the assets owned by private pension plans. This is false. Congress has already spent the past excess of taxes over benefits and has simply given the trust fund IOUs. These IOUs are called U.S. Treasury bonds, and they are nothing more than promises by the U.S. Treasury to levy taxes on someone to pay benefits. When it is time for the trust fund to redeem the IOUs it holds, Congress will have to

1. raise taxes;
2. cut spending on other programs; or
3. borrow more money to raise the funds.

But this would be true even if there were *no* Treasury bonds in the trust fund: all Social Security benefits ultimately must be paid for out of taxes. So, whatever might have been intended for the trust fund, the only asset actually backing that fund is nothing more and nothing less than an obligation of Americans—you—to pay taxes in the future.

## Myth 4: Social Security Will Be There for You

Social Security was a great deal for Ida Mae Fuller, who, in 1940, became the first person to receive a regular Social Security pension. She had paid a total of $25 in Social Security taxes before she retired. By the time she died in 1975 at the age of 100, she had received benefits totaling $23,000. And although Ida Mae did better than most, the *average* annual real rate of return for those early retirees was an astounding 135 percent *per year*. (That is, after adjusting for inflation, every initial $100 in taxes paid yielded $135 *per year* during each and every year of that person's retirement.)

People retiring more recently have not done quite so well, but everyone who retired by about 1970 has received a far better return from Social Security than could likely have been obtained from any other investment. These higher benefits relative to contributions were made possible because *at each point in time, current retirees are paid benefits out of the taxes paid by those who are currently working.* Social Security is a **pay-as-you-go system;** it is not like a true retirement plan in which participants pay into a fund and receive benefits according to what they have paid in and how much that fund has cumulatively earned. So, as long as Social Security was pulling in enough new people each year, the system could offer benefits that were high relative to taxes paid. But membership in Social Security is no longer growing so fast, and the number of retirees is growing faster. Moreover, today's added trickle of new retirees soon will become tomorrow's flood, as the Baby Boomer generation exits the workforce. The result is bad news all around.

One way to think about the problem facing us—which is chiefly a problem facing you—is to contemplate the number of retirees each worker must support. In 1945, forty-two workers shared the burden of one Social Security recipient. By 1960, nine workers had to pick up the tab for each person collecting

Social Security. Today, the burden of a retiree is spread out among a bit over four workers. Within twenty-five years, fewer than three workers will be available to pay the Social Security benefits due each recipient.

The coming tax bill for all of this will be staggering. If we *immediately* raised Social Security (payroll) taxes from 15.3 percent to a bit over 19 percent—more than a 24 percent increase—and kept them there for the next 75 years or so, the system's revenues probably would be large enough to meet its obligations. But this would be the largest tax increase in U.S. history—which makes it extremely unlikely that it will occur. Yet every day that Congress delays, the situation gets worse. If Congress waits until 2030 to raise taxes, they will have to be increased by more than 50 percent. Indeed, some commentators are predicting that without fundamental reforms to the system, payroll taxes *alone* will have to be hiked to 25 percent of wages—in addition to regular federal, state, and local income taxes, of course.

And what form are these reforms likely to take? Well, rules will specify that people must be older before they become eligible for Social Security benefits. Existing legislation already is inching the age for full benefits up to 67 from its previous 65. Almost certainly, this age threshold will be hiked again, perhaps to 70. Moreover, it is likely that all Social Security benefits (rather than just a portion) eventually will be subject to federal income taxes. It is even possible that some high-income individuals—you, perhaps—will be declared ineligible for benefits because their income from other sources is too high.

So, what does all this mean for you? Well, technically, a Social Security system likely will be in existence when you retire—although the retirement age surely will be higher than today, and benefits will be scaled back significantly. It is also likely that, strictly speaking, the Social Security Trust Fund will still be around when you hit whatever is then the relevant minimum age for benefits. But whatever else happens to the Social Security system between now and your retirement, you can be secure in your knowledge of one thing: you will be getting a much bigger tax bill from the federal government to pay for it.

## For Critical Analysis

1. Where has all of the Social Security money gone?
2. People over the age of 65 have been highly successful in protecting and enhancing the real benefits they receive from Social Security. All of this has come at the expense of other people in society, particularly young people. What do you think explains the ability of older people to win political battles with younger people?
3. Analyze how each of the hypothetical policy changes listed below would affect people's decision to retire. Would the change induce people to retire sooner or later?

   a. an increase in the age at which one can receive full Social Security benefits (currently ages 65 to 67, depending on the year in which a person was born)
   b. a decrease in the fraction (currently 75 percent) of full benefits that one can receive if retirement occurs at age 62
   c. an increase in the Medicare eligibility age from its current level of 65
   d. an increase to 100 percent from its current 85 percent in the fraction of Social Security benefits that is subject to the federal income tax.

# 14

# *Tax Cuts: When They Matter, When They Don't*

All modern presidents have one thing in common: they promise to cut taxes or at least not raise them. Some presidents have even succeeded in keeping their word, for we have seen numerous tax cuts over the last half-century. From a **fiscal policy** point of view, not all tax cuts are the same, though. That is, some tax cuts have had relatively little effect on unemployment and economic growth, while others have had significant effects. What we want to know is, why aren't all tax cuts created equal?

## First Things First—The Importance of the Margin

In economics we say that choices are always made at *the margin*. What this means is that people react to whatever changes their *incentive structure* in terms of **marginal benefits** and **marginal costs.** If the government were to announce a one-time-only **lump-sum tax cut** of, say, $1,000 per family, little, if any, change in the incentive structure facing consumers, savers, and investors would occur. Why not? Because the one-time-only cut in taxes would not change the marginal benefit or marginal cost of any of the activities of consumers, savers, or investors.

What is important to the incentives—and thus the behavior—of individuals is whether their actions can affect their income, net of taxes. As you probably know, the more taxable income you make, the higher your **tax bracket,** and thus the higher the marginal tax rate you pay on the last dollar of income earned. So, if you are a single person and your taxable income goes from, say, $25,000 to $40,000, your marginal tax rate will jump from, say, 15 percent to 25 percent.

As the following table shows for a recent year, as your taxable income goes up, you jump into higher and higher tax brackets. In general, to make sensible choices about working, people need to evaluate the marginal benefit of earning more income compared to the marginal cost, where costs are measured in terms of added effort and additional forgone leisure activities. The higher the marginal tax rate, the lower the marginal benefits from working, because less income is kept by the person who earned it. So, as marginal tax rates rise, the incentive to work is reduced, because the marginal benefits of work are reduced.

## Marginal Tax Rates for Single Taxpayers

| Taxable Income | Marginal Tax Rate |
|---|---|
| $0–$7,150 | 10.0% |
| $7,151–$29,050 | 15.0% |
| $29,051–$70,350 | 25.0% |
| $70,351–$146,750 | 28.0% |
| $146,751–$319,100 | 33.0% |
| Over $319,100 | 35.0% |

## Next—The Importance of Permanence

A second issue that must be considered when thinking about tax cuts is their permanence—or lack thereof. In general, people are forward-looking creatures. They consider not just what is happening today, but also what is likely to happen later in the year and even several years into the future. Thus, for two reasons, a tax cut that is expected to be short-lived is much different from one that is expected to be long-lived or permanent.

The first reason is that a temporary tax cut can induce people to make temporary changes in their behavior that have very little sustained effect. For example, if income taxes are cut this year but people know they will be raised again next year, people will respond quite simply: they'll work more this year and work less next year. Politicians may make headlines by pointing out the extra employment and output this year, but the reality is that over the longer haul, little will have changed.

The second reason permanence is important has to do with investment. People invest when they get an education, and firms invest when they build new plants or buy new equipment. Investments yield income over long periods of time, and so people worry about the long-run taxes on that income. A permanent tax cut will raise the marginal benefits of investment far more than will a short-lived tax cut, because it has a greater impact on the total value of the tax bill.

## Permanent and Marginal

The upshot of all this is quite simple. A short-lived tax cut or a one-time **tax rebate** is unlikely to affect incentives on the margin and, thus, is unlikely to affect people's behavior. But a permanent reduction in *marginal* income tax rates can have substantial effects on how much people are willing to work, save, and invest. Indeed, there is considerable evidence that when marginal tax rates at the highest levels have been reduced, Americans earning those relatively high incomes have responded by working more, saving more, and investing more.

Consider also that those who take risks in our economy—**entrepreneurs**—are sensitive to the potential net reward to such risk taking. Higher net rewards lead to more risk taking and certainly, in the long run, to greater economic growth.

A recent study conducted in France examined the implications of the French tax system. Researchers calculated what Bill Gates, founder and chairman of the largest software company in the world, Microsoft, would be worth today if he had started that company in France. Had Gates been a Frenchman and started Microsoft in France, he would have faced much higher marginal tax rates on both his personal income and the gains to his investments. The researchers estimated that Gates's **net worth** would be about 80 percent *less* than what it actually is today in the United States. The average French person's response to this information was, so what? The leftover 20 percent of many billions of dollars is still a lot of wealth. An economist's response is quite different. Bill Gates, or anybody else taking risks, would have taken fewer business risks (and worked fewer nights and weekends and taken more vacations) had marginal tax rates been as high as they have been (and currently are) in France.

## Three Cases of Marginal Tax Cuts and Their Results

During three important periods in the twentieth century, U.S. presidents significantly lowered marginal tax rates. The first cuts were the Coolidge-Mellon marginal tax rate cuts of the 1920s. The result: the Roaring Twenties. The second were the tax cuts pushed by President John F. Kennedy in the early 1960s and implemented somewhat reluctantly by Congress after Kennedy's assassination. The result: the prosperous 1960s. The last major marginal personal income tax cut was enacted under the leadership of President Ronald Reagan in the 1980s. The result: the boom that lasted from 1983 to 1990.

Critics of this analysis of the effects of marginal tax rate cuts point out that many other things were happening in both the United States and the world during these three very different periods. Nevertheless, the fact remains that one variable was the same in each period—major cuts in federal marginal personal income tax rates.

## The Problem with Backward-Looking Windfalls

Presidents have, at times, believed they could "jump-start" a slowly moving or stagnating economy by sending out tax rebate checks from the U.S. Treasury. Indeed, rebates have been used several times in the past twenty years. The result of tax rebates has always been nil. Specifically, very little change in unemployment and in the rate of economic growth has ever occurred after the issuance of a tax rebate.

The reasons are pretty obvious. Tax rebates are backward looking—they are based on *past* income and work effort, both of which are out of the individual's control. None of the marginal benefits or marginal costs associated with work, saving, or investing is affected. Moreover, such tax cuts are temporary; even if they somehow could be linked to future actions (such as by offering a tax rebate on income earned over the next year), there would be no permanent effects on incentives. Most notably, any change in incentive to save or invest would be minimal, implying that the impact on economic growth would be negligible.

## Tax Cuts and Phase-Outs

Phase-outs for **personal exemptions** and **itemized deductions** (e.g., charitable contributions and mortgage interest payments) started in 1990 as a seemingly innocent way to raise federal government tax revenues without appearing to do so. Under the phase-out provisions of the current tax law, as you earn more taxable income, after a certain level, the federal government reduces (phases out) your personal exemptions and itemized deductions. The current Internal Revenue Code slowly, but surely, takes away certain tax breaks as taxable income goes up. In 2004, for example, taxpayers filing single or joint returns started losing their itemized deductions and personal exemptions when their adjusted gross income exceeded $142,700.

The existence of phase-outs leads to higher *de facto* marginal tax rates, and Americans are not stupid. Those earning higher incomes understand quite clearly that their marginal tax rates are higher than those listed in the government tax tables. Why? Because the phase-outs for itemized deductions and personal exemptions effectively increase marginal tax rates by increasing taxable income by more than the person's additional earnings.

On balance, the phase-outs add an extra 1 to 2 percentage points to marginal tax rates at the upper end.

The continued existence of phase-outs dampens the potential effectiveness of any cuts in federal marginal income tax rates, such as those implemented in 2003. For higher-income-earning individuals, any given reduction in marginal tax rates is less because of phase-outs. Higher-income-earning individuals react accordingly, correctly treating the supposed tax cut as being less than the politicians say it is—and working and investing less than one might otherwise expect.

## Income versus Payroll Tax Cuts

Most proposed and enacted tax cuts have involved federal personal income taxes. The federal government, though, likes to play a little game with its tax revenues. It labels some taxes as income taxes, but it labels other taxes as **payroll taxes.** These payroll taxes are supposedly used for Social Security, disability, and Medicare expenses. To keep the illusion going, the law says that employers and employees share payroll taxes equally.

There is a saying that a rose is a rose; among economists, the corresponding saying is that a dollar is a dollar. These sayings mean one thing only: it doesn't matter what label a government puts on a tax; what matters is tax revenues. When the government spends funds, recipients and taxpayers care not a hoot from which particular tax revenue accounts those funds are supposedly derived. Whether Medicare payments come out of a fund labeled "payroll taxes" or are paid from an account called "general fund," there is no difference to the economy. What matters to the incentives and thus the behavior of taxpayers are the dollars left on the margin after the government collects taxes.

Today, the top 50 percent of income earners in America pay approximately 96 percent of all federal income taxes. Almost 50 percent of income earners pay *no* federal personal income taxes. Not surprisingly, when President George W. Bush presented his 2003 plan to reduce federal income taxes, 50 percent of

Americans polled did not believe that federal income taxes were too high. Why should they? Almost none of them actually *pay* any federal income taxes.

In contrast, virtually anybody who is self-employed or works for a company pays payroll taxes. When payroll taxes were instituted over seventy years ago, they represented a mere 1 percent of federal tax revenues. Today, they represent about 35 percent. Because so many people actually pay payroll taxes, some economists have called for a reduction in these taxes. University of Texas economist Daniel Hamermesh estimated that a 10-percentage-point reduction in payroll taxes would lead to a short-term 3 percent increase in employment and a long-term 10 percent increase in employment in the United States. His analysis explicitly uses marginal thinking. The reward to working would increase permanently and the cost of hiring would decrease permanently. The obvious result: a larger supply of workers and a greater demand for workers.

Will we see a reduction in payroll taxes soon? Probably not. As long as the myth that we need to have a separate fund for Social Security and Medicare continues to dominate thinking in Congress, the payroll tax will remain sacrosanct. In fact, as we note in Chapter 13, payroll taxes will probably continue to rise in order to "fund" Social Security and Medicare benefit payments. Despite the adverse incentive effects of these taxes, no politician in his or her right mind wants to be accused of "tampering" with Social Security or Medicare.

## For Critical Analysis

1. When Congress analyzes proposed federal tax cuts, it often issues statements that such cuts will cost the U.S. Treasury so many billions of dollars per year. Is this analysis the same as when a corporation estimates how much it will cost to institute a new environmental program? Why or why not?
2. Sometimes Congress passes tax cuts that won't go into effect until many years in the future. Do you believe that such future tax cuts have any effect on the economy today? Why or why not?

3. The Jobs & Growth Tax Relief and Reconciliation Act of 2003 lowered federal taxes in a variety of ways. A few of these ways include (i) a one-time tax rebate, unrelated to current or future income; (ii) a reduction in marginal income tax rates applicable to people at all levels of income; and (iii) a reduction in the capital gains tax rate (applicable to increases in the market value of assets, such as corporate stocks or land). Analyze how each of these provisions affects (or does not affect) the incentives to work and to invest.

# 15

## Simplifying the Federal Tax System (Don't Hold Your Breath)

Although the dictum that "nothing is certain except death and taxes" seems ingrained in our society today, it wasn't always so. Indeed, except briefly during the Civil War, the United States had no federal income tax until after the adoption of the Sixteenth Amendment in 1913. As one lawmaker pointed out during the debates at that time, with a federal income tax, "a hand from Washington will stretch out to every man's house." The Sixteenth Amendment passed nonetheless.

Despite the intense debate over its initiation, the federal income tax was not so onerous in the beginning. Congress exempted individual incomes below about $50,000 in today's dollars and married couples' incomes below about $65,000. Moreover, tax rates were low, and the design of the system was quite simple, as reflected in the table on the next page, which shows the very first system we had in 1913.

In addition to imposing a low burden even on those who paid taxes, the federal income tax code in the beginning was easy to understand and applied to very few Americans. Those who did pay filled out a simple one-page form. Consider now how far we have come from "the good old days."

## The Original Federal Tax Code, In Modern Terms

| Tax Rate | Income Level in 1913 | Equivalent Income Level in 2004 |
|---|---|---|
| 1% | Up to $20,000 | Up to $338,350 |
| 2% | $20,001–$50,000 | $338,351–$845,900 |
| 3% | $50,001–$75,000 | $845,901–$1,268,800 |
| 4% | $75,001–$100,000 | $1,268,801–$1,691,750 |
| 5% | $100,001–$250,000 | $1,691,751–$4,229,400 |
| 6% | $250,001–$500,000 | $4,229,401–$8,458,800 |
| 7% | Over $500,000 | Over $8,458,800 |

## Our Complex Internal Revenue Code

Just try to grasp the following passage from a page out of the Internal Revenue Code—a passage that is not at all atypical:

> Line 20 b(1).—You must complete this line if there is a gain on Form 4797, Line 3; a loss on 4797, Line 12; and a loss on Form 4684, Line 35, Column (b)(ii). Enter on this line and on Schedule A (Form 1040) Line 22, the smaller of the loss on Form 4797, Line 12; or the loss on Form 4684, Line 35, Column (b)(ii). To figure which loss is smaller, treat both losses as positive numbers.

Now, if you can figure that out, you are probably a certified public accountant with many years of experience. It's not just taxpayers who think the tax code is complicated. Just a few years ago, the head of the Internal Revenue Service asked for 30,000 more agents because "the tax system continues to grow in complexity, while the resource base of the IRS is not growing."

Why is the Internal Revenue Code so complicated? The problem is that Congress enacts change after change in our tax laws, layering new provisions on top of old ones, seemingly without much regard for the web it is weaving. From 1998 through 2002, Congress enacted over 300 such changes. Then in 2003, Congress went through the tax code from top to bottom, making hundreds *more* changes. To understand our current complicated tax code, it helps to appreciate the action-reaction syndrome.

## Action-Reaction Syndrome

People are not assessed a lump-sum tax each year; each family does not just pay $1,000 or $10,000 or $20,000. Rather, individuals and businesses pay taxes based on tax rates. The higher the **tax rate**—the action on the part of the government—the greater the public's reaction to that tax rate, either by trying to hide income or by attempting to convince Congress to lighten the burden. It is all a matter of costs and benefits.

If the highest tax rate (called your **marginal tax rate**) you pay on the income you make is 15 percent, then any method you can use to reduce your taxable income by one dollar saves you 15 cents in tax liabilities that you owe the federal government. Therefore, those individuals paying a 15 percent rate have a relatively small incentive to avoid paying taxes. But consider individuals who were faced with a tax rate of 94 percent in the 1940s. They had a tremendous incentive to find legal ways to reduce their taxable income. For every dollar of income that was somehow deemed nontaxable, these taxpayers would reduce their tax liabilities by 94 cents.

One way that individuals and corporations facing high tax rates react is by making concerted attempts to get Congress to add **loopholes** to the tax laws that allow them to reduce their taxable incomes. Indeed, it is commonplace that when Congress changes the Internal Revenue Code to impose higher tax rates on high incomes, it also provides for more loopholes, either immediately or soon thereafter. For example, special provisions enable investors in oil and gas wells to reduce their taxable incomes. Other loopholes allow people to shift income from one year to the next. Still other loopholes permit individuals to avoid some taxes completely by forming corporations outside the United States. Every loophole means another paragraph or page in the tax code. Furthermore, because loopholes lower tax receipts, the tax rate imposed on other people has to be that much higher, if the government wishes to collect a specific amount of tax revenues.

There are literally thousands of loopholes scattered throughout the tax code, garnered by hundreds of **interest groups.** As long as one group of taxpayers sees a specific benefit from getting the law changed and that benefit means a lot of money per individual, the interest group will lobby aggressively and support the election and reelection of members of Congress who will push for the loopholes desired by that group. If the benefits from influencing tax legislation are high enough, the affected parties will exert such influence—and will likely get their way. The result: a few more paragraphs or pages in the tax code, and a slightly higher tax rate imposed on the rest of the populace.

## Some Possible Simplifications in the Federal Tax System

Every several years, presidential candidates, candidates for Congress, and economists in and out of academia consider alternatives to the current federal tax system. Here are some of those possibilities:

- *Value-added tax*—This is a type of sales tax, currently used throughout Europe, which involves taxing only the value that is added at each stage of production. By the time this tax gets around to the ultimate consumer, it averages around 20 percent in Europe. Yale Law Professor Michael Graetz has calculated that a 15 percent value-added tax could be used to eliminate the federal income tax for families earning less than $100,000 a year. Those earning over $100,000 a year would still have to pay some income taxes, but at a rate (25 percent) lower than today and under a greatly simplified system.

  Of course, a proposal such as this might present a few political problems. Would health-care expenditures be subject to the value-added tax? Probably not, because senior citizens (who consume most of the nation's health-care resources) would convince politicians that this would impose an "unfair" burden on them. The result would be a few more paragraphs or pages added to the code and a slightly higher value-added tax on everything else. What about housing expenditures—would they be subject to the value-added tax, too? Probably not, because the housing industry's lobbyists are so strong that they would likely get an exemption, and we would get a few more pages in the tax code. Of course, every time a new exemption was applied, the value-added tax would have to be raised—which would add to the pressure for more loopholes. Moreover, although young people might like the system, retired people would probably object to the implicit "double taxation" they would face under such a scheme. After all, today's working people would get lower income taxes in return for the new value-added tax. But retirees, who paid income taxes throughout their working careers, would now simply be getting stuck with the new value-added tax. Politicians would probably agree that this would be unfair, and so a few more paragraphs or pages would be added to the new tax code, and the rate paid by young people would have to be raised—just a bit, of course.

- **National sales tax**—A straightforward national sales tax sounds simple. Eliminate the federal income tax and simply tax everything that is sold to consumers. The problem is that such a national sales tax would have to be over 20 percent to start with. Then, if food, clothing, and health-care costs were exempted (perhaps on the grounds that taxes on such items would impose an unfair burden on the poor and the elderly), the national sales tax would have to be even higher. Another issue is how we would transition to a national sales tax. A massive one-time shift to the new system would likely generate huge swings in working and spending behavior, as people tried to take advantage of the switch from a tax on earnings to a tax on spending. Moreover, some would argue that low-income earners would be hit harder by a sales tax because they spend a higher percentage of their income than do high-income earners. Politicians responding to this plea would have to add only a few more pages to the tax code and perhaps impose just a slightly higher sales tax on those not exempt.

- *Flat tax*—This concept has been around for decades. At its core it is simple, just like the alternatives mentioned above. Exempt all income up to some amount, such as $50,000, and tax all other income at one rate, say, 17 percent. There would be no deductions at all. There are many reasons why such a tax system has not been enacted and likely never will be. The first claim made against it is that the rich benefit more than the poor, which is an argument that no politician wants to ignore. A second reason this proposal can't get off the ground is that the housing industry has been very effective at lobbying against it. Firms in this industry have opposed the flat tax for years because the current exemption for interest payments on **mortgages** serves to increase the demand for housing.

## Who Really Pays the Federal Income Tax?

Over the last several decades, fewer and fewer Americans have been paying the federal income tax. Furthermore, the richest Americans are paying an ever-increasing percentage of the total federal income taxes paid. For example, those with incomes over $500,000 account for only 0.5 percent of all U.S. taxpayers, but they pay over 28 percent of total federal taxes. That means that fewer than 600,000 Americans pay over one-fourth of the $1 trillion of federal personal income taxes collected.

Moving down the income ladder, the pattern repeats itself. The top 1 percent of income earners pay 37.4 percent of all federal taxes. The top 5 percent of income earners in the United States pay more than 50 percent of total federal tax revenues. (To get into the top 5 percent, you have to earn an adjusted gross income of about $140,000.) And it gets worse: the top 50 percent of income earners in the United States pay 96 percent of total federal taxes. Every year, over one-fourth of all tax filers show no taxes owed. Another 25 percent of working Americans earn income but don't file tax returns at all.

These data tell us nothing about the "fairness" of the current tax system, of course. But the data do tell us that about half of Americans don't care very much about tax relief or about simplifying the tax system, because that means tax relief or tax simplification for everybody else. In fact, a growing proportion of Americans have become detached from the federal personal income tax system and indeed even from the cost of the federal government, because they don't pay the tab.

The moral of the story is that when it comes to simplifying the tax system, don't hold your breath.

## For Critical Analysis

1. Which groups in society would be hurt the most if we went to a simplified tax system that did not require much effort on the part of taxpayers to comply with it?
2. How do members of Congress benefit from our complicated federal tax system? (HINT: To whom must those seeking tax exemptions or benefits go in order to get them enacted?)
3. How does the political balance in favor of tax cuts versus tax increases change as the proportion of the populace who pays taxes changes? For example, would the balance of opinions in favor of a tax cut change if 96 percent of taxes were paid by 96 percent of the people, compared to the current 96 percent being paid by only 50 percent of the people? How does the evenness with which income taxes are levied affect the incentives to vote among people at different income levels?

# Raising the Debt Ceiling— What's a Few Trillion Dollars, More or Less?

Almost every year since the end of World War II, the U.S. Congress has engaged in a debate over raising the U.S. **public debt** ceiling. Although Congress took a debate break during the surplus years of 1999 and 2000, the issue reheated with the resurgence of federal spending deficits in the early 2000s. Not long before the 2004 elections, the U.S. Treasury Department asked this august body of lawmakers to raise the public debt ceiling to $8.1 trillion. If that sounds like a lot, it is. Indeed, it takes everyone in the economy working full-time for about seven months to produce new goods and services (called **gross domestic product,** or **GDP**) worth that much. But before you join one of those protest groups that have declared war on U.S. government debt, consider a few "corrections" that have to be made to this $8.1 trillion figure before it can be viewed in proper perspective.

## First Things First—How the Government Accumulates Debt

You know how you accumulate debt—you spend more than you earn. You accumulate debt through credit card use, borrowing for a house or car purchase, or even borrowing to pay for your education. In this sense, your household finances are no different than those of the federal government. Whenever the federal government spends more than it receives from its revenue sources—personal income taxes, corporate income taxes, excise taxes, taxes on imports—it has to borrow to make up the difference. The federal government has spent more than it received in all but a few years since the end of World War II. Thus, it should not surprise you that just about every year, Congress has had to raise the U.S. debt ceiling. If it had not—that is, without the grease of borrowed funds—the gears of the federal government would have slowed down considerably.

So, the U.S. public, or national, debt is simply the accumulated deficits that the federal government has racked up since its beginning. Notwithstanding this fact, that $8.1 trillion debt ceiling needs a closer look before we can decide what has really happened with our federal government's finances.

## The Difference between the Gross and the Net Public Debt

Let's say your household consists of you and three other family members. During the year, suppose you and other members of the household borrow from and lend funds to each other. At the same time, imagine that, as a household, you have borrowed from the outside to finance the purchase of a house. During the year, your internal borrowings may have been, say, $5,000. Your external borrowing to purchase the house may have been $100,000. What does your household as a whole really worry about? Clearly, only the borrowings from the outside. Your household's gross debt is $105,000, but your net debt is only $100,000. It is the latter sum that measures your household's true indebtedness.

The federal government acts the same way as the hypothetical household just described. It has numerous interagency borrowings; that is, various branches of the federal government borrow other branches. Of course, the federal government also borrows from the outside—from individuals, corporations, and foreigners. The debt ceiling of $8.1 trillion applies to the **gross public debt** of the federal government. This number is largely meaningless, although it is reported in the press all the time. When interagency government borrowings are subtracted from this number, we obtain the **net public debt**. Look at the table below to see the difference.

This table reveals that, once we net out the federal government's debt to itself, the growth in debt is much more modest than one would otherwise think. Even so, we are still not getting a number that tells us much about the true burden of the federal government's indebtedness.

## Some Relevant Comparisons of the Public Debt

If your net indebtedness to the outside world was $100,000, should you be worried? The only way you could answer this question is to compare your net indebtedness to your capacity to repay that debt—measured perhaps by your annual income or your total assets. If you made $2 million a year after taxes or had assets of $50 million, you certainly would not worry too much about a debt of $100,000. The same reasoning applies to the federal government. One way to see if the net public debt is getting out of hand is to compare it to the annual

### Gross and Net Public Debt, Selected Years, 1950–2006 (Billions of Dollars)

| Year | Gross Public Debt | Net Public Debt | Ratio (Net/Gross) |
|------|-------------------|-----------------|-------------------|
| 1950 | 259.9 | 219.0 | 0.84 |
| 1960 | 290.5 | 236.8 | 0.82 |
| 1970 | 380.9 | 283.2 | 0.74 |
| 1980 | 909.1 | 711.9 | 0.78 |
| 1990 | 3,206.6 | 2,411.8 | 0.75 |
| 2006* | 8,029.0 | 4,175.0 | 0.52 |

* Estimates

income of the United States as a whole, or the GDP as it is normally called. In 1946, right after the end of World War II, the net national debt was $242 billion, and the GDP was $223 billion. Thus, the net public debt was 109 percent of the GDP. In 1970, the ratio of net public debt to the GDP was 28 percent, and in 2005 it was 35 percent.

So, should you be worried about the increased indebtedness of your federal government? Probably not.

Yet another way to examine the importance of the net federal public debt is to (1) correct it for inflation and (2) correct it for increases in population. In terms of 2005 dollars, the real net public debt per capita was $13,485 in 1946, $4,932 in 1970, and $13,415 in 2005. Although the jump in this figure since 1970 looks large, it must be remembered that we are much richer now than in 1970 and, thus, are better able to repay the debt. For example, **real per capita GDP** has more than doubled over this same period. Again we ask: Should these figures concern you? And again we answer: probably not.

## Reasons for Recent Increases in the Net Public Debt

During the Clinton administration (1993–2001), ever-increasing federal surpluses were predicted. Eventually, in 1999 and 2000, those surpluses materialized. Since then, there have been only federal budget deficits. There are several reasons for those federal deficits. The first is the economic recession of 2001, caused by a mix of stringent monetary policy and the meltdown in the technology sector of the stock market in 2000. During any recession, there is a slowdown in the economy and, consequently, a slowdown in federal government revenues from individual and corporate taxes. Because the federal government does not automatically cut back on its expenditures during recessions (and, actually, often increases its expenditures), recessions lead to increasing federal government deficits.

The second reason for higher deficits lies in the new fight against terrorism and the war with Iraq. Since the attacks on

New York City and Washington, D.C., on September 11, 2001, and the subsequent wars in Afghanistan and Iraq, the federal government has spent more on fighting terrorism and on the defense budget than in prior years. So, the government budget has been hit with a double whammy—reduced revenues during the recent recession and unexpected increased expenditures to fight terrorism worldwide.

A third cause of the increased deficits involves the tax cuts that were passed in 2001 and 2003 at the behest of the Bush administration. Those in Congress who are worried about increased federal deficits have decried those tax cuts, arguing that they are responsible for the rising federal deficits. Although it is highly doubtful that those tax reductions were responsible for much of the increased deficits in 2001 and 2002, by 2003 they surely had begun to show up in the federal deficit.

So the bottom line of our story is twofold. First, most of the newspaper headlines about increases in the federal debt ceiling are so much wasted ink: realistically appraised, the net debt situation of the federal government is little different than it was thirty years ago, and much better than it was sixty years ago. Second, although Congress talks a good game, the reality of politics prevents it from doing much about the reality of the federal deficit except occasionally. Instead, year-to-year changes in the deficit (and thus government debt) are driven chiefly by forces beyond congressional control, whether those forces are economic or geopolitical.

## For Critical Analysis

1. When you borrow, you have to pay interest on the borrowings. So, too, does the federal government. Who ultimately pays the interest on the U.S. net public debt?
2. If you were running a large business, would you necessarily want to eliminate all of your debt if you were making profits every year? (HINT: Virtually every publicly held U.S. company has outstanding corporate debt, even after years and years of profitability.)

**3.** Until 1917, every time the U.S. Treasury wanted to issue any bonds (borrow any money) on behalf of the federal government, it had to ask Congress for permission. In that year, Congress switched to our current system in which Congress sets a "debt ceiling" every few years: as long as the total public debt of the federal government does not exceed this ceiling, the U.S. Treasury can borrow whatever money is required to finance expenditures. In 2003, the Bush administration argued that the debt ceiling should be abolished and replaced with a system in which (i) the U.S. Treasury borrows whatever is needed to meet Congressionally-approved spending, and (ii) Congress would examine the U.S. Treasury's performance every four or five years to ensure that it is doing what Congress wants it to. Why would a president want the debt ceiling eliminated? Why might Congress want to keep it in place? Because Congress can change the debt ceiling any time it wants, does the ceiling really constrain federal spending or borrowing?

# *Bad Accounting by Uncle Sam*

In the early 2000s, accounting scandals at a number of major corporations made headlines for months at a time. For example, Enron, a major energy-trading firm, was discovered to have moved its liabilities to extremely complex, not-easily-discoverable, offshore partnerships. So, rather than making hundreds of millions of dollars of **profits**—as reported to the public—it was actually incurring massive losses. Enron went bankrupt and $62 billion of shareholder value disappeared, virtually overnight. Similarly, WorldCom, a major telecommunications firm, inappropriately spread out the costs of current operations, trying to disguise them as capital expenditures. Doing this resulted in grossly inflated profits. When word got out, WorldCom, too, went bankrupt.

The president and Congress reacted swiftly to these embarrassing scandals by passing a new law aimed at "truth in accounting." As a result, chief executive officers (CEOs) and chief financial officers (CFOs) of most **publicly traded corporations** now must actually sign the documents that contain all accounting information released to the public and to regulatory agencies. When they sign, they are attesting to the truth and accuracy of the numbers that will be released to the public. They can be fined and even sent to prison if the accounting later turns out to have been fraudulent.

Well, if personal accountability is good for corporate America, why not for the U.S. government? In other words, why not have personal accountability for those who make accounting projections for the federal government?

## All Those Projections Have Always Proved False

When Bill Clinton was in the White House (1993–2001), after a few years of being president, he and his staff released projections indicating that the federal government would run a surplus of $10 trillion over the next ten years. After a few years, however, the same federal accountants cut that surplus to $5 trillion. When George W. Bush became president, he started off by projecting a ten-year budget surplus of $5.6 trillion. He argued that his proposed spending programs plus a proposed tax cut could all be funded easily with this projected surplus. Some of his pet programs included a prescription drug benefit for Medicare recipients and increased federal spending for education.

That was then. By early 2002, the $5.6 trillion ten-year surplus had shrunk to less than half a trillion dollars. And only a year after that, the federal government was projecting multi-trillion dollar **budget deficits** instead of surpluses. So, how can the official budget projections change so dramatically in such a short period of time? Is it possible that presidents and their staffs "fiddle" with their economic assumptions to paint a rosier picture than will really occur? In other words, does the U.S. government engage in some of the accounting tricks that have been used by the Enrons and WorldComs of the business world? Unfortunately, often the answer is "yes."

## The Assumptions Used in
## Federal Government Accounting

When a president and his staff make a budget projection over a ten-year period, they must use certain assumptions. They have to assume a certain rate of growth of the GDP over that period. They also have to assume something about how much different parts of the federal budget will grow each year.

Many people accuse each administration, whether Republican or Democrat, of routinely making assumptions that are, well, absurd. After looking at some of the facts, it is hard to ignore such accusations. For example, the Bush administration, in making its projections, assumed that **real federal discretionary spending** would remain constant over the ensuing ten years. With normal real economic growth, that would mean that real discretionary spending relative to GDP would fall by 20 percent. Such a decline has *never* happened in modern times. So, the question arises, why would it happen over the ten years following the Bush projections? The answer is that almost certainly it would not, and the president and his staff just as certainly knew that it wouldn't. Therefore, the administration's ten-year projections were far too optimistic.

There is something else quite unusual about the ten-year projections of all recent administrations. To understand the accounting problem to which we are referring, consider the modern corporation. If it knows that it has a **long-term liability** that it must pay, it sets aside financial reserves today to pay off that liability. These **reserves** are recorded on the company's books as a cost, and they therefore reduce reported profits. For example, in 2002 and 2003 many major corporations, such as General Motors and IBM, set aside reserves for their pension plans, because those plans had lost so much value during the stock market decline in 2001 and 2002. Consequently, because of the extra reserve set-asides, the reported profits of these firms fell.

There is a big long-term liability looming for the federal government. It is called Social Security and Medicare, and the liability can be measured in trillions of dollars (that's right, trillions, not billions). Nonetheless, the federal government's ten-year projections completely ignore these growing long-term liabilities. Actually, the accounting practices are even worse than that. The really big Social Security liabilities will be payable more than ten years in the future. Between now and then, these two programs are temporarily bringing in more funds than they are spending. These extra funds are supposed to help pay the bills for these programs down the road. But for the last twenty years or so, the official budget projections have counted this cash surplus for Medicare and Social Security as though it were net income, rather than being only a partial down payment against huge *future* liabilities. This certainly helps make the presidential projections look better—regardless of who that president is—but it doesn't reveal to the taxpayer what really is going on.

## The Sea of Government-Backed Debt

The misleading accounting practices of the federal government extend even further. For example, nowhere in any U.S. president's ten-year projections will you see a reserve for the possible failure of **government-backed debt.** Time and again over the years, the federal government has agreed to bail out any number of companies that have issued debt and later been unable to repay it in full. The most recent candidate for this treatment is the Federal National Mortgage Association, quaintly called Fannie Mae. This U.S. mortgage company giant is privately owned. Nonetheless, the U.S. government originally founded Fannie Mae, and there is no doubt in financial markets that U.S. taxpayers are implicitly its ultimate backers, through the federal government.

How the federal government came to create Fannie Mae, and to implicitly guarantee its debt, has its origins in the idea that a nation of private homeowners is more civic minded and politically stable. In effect, federal backing for mortgages came about because of the argument that home ownership generates **positive externalities**—because supposedly homeowners (as opposed to renters) are more responsible citizens. Fannie Mae sees its job as reducing mortgage interest rates to create more "affordable" housing. (As it turns out, most of this "affordability" is enjoyed by middle- and upper-income homeowners, rather than by lower-income individuals who can't afford to buy a home—but that is another story.)

In the process of subsidizing bigger and better homes for those who can afford them, Fannie Mae has racked up total liabilities of $1.8 trillion (again, that's trillion, not billion). Given that Fannie Mae's net assets are less than one-half of 1 percent of its $1.8 trillion of liabilities, the federal government—which is to say, you, the taxpayer of the future—is potentially on the hook quite seriously. But you will find no reserves for Fannie Mae's possible **insolvency** in the ten-year projections that each administration presents.

One interesting upshot of the WorldCom and Enron scandals of the early 2000s is that after the dust settled, it was found that the overwhelming majority of all private firms had actually been following very sound accounting practices. Perhaps this is partly because there is little doubt that if a privately owned corporation engaged in the accounting trickery that is common practice for the federal government, that corporation would be pummeled in the press and deserted by investors. Given the recently enacted accounting reform legislation we mentioned earlier, there is now even less chance of such irregularities, because the CEO and CFO of such a corporation would soon be headed for federal prison. If you can figure out why the federal government is allowed to get away with this—by journalists and voters alike—let us know. Meanwhile, expect more of the same behavior, whether Republicans or Democrats are in office.

## For Critical Analysis

1. If you compared ten-year federal government budget projections over time with what actually happened, what do you think you would discover?

2. A publicly held corporation, at least in the short run, may have an incentive to play with its books to show higher profits. That incentive, of course, is a higher stock value. What is the incentive of the federal government to present the equivalent—rosy ten-year projections for the federal budget?

3. Is it realistic to hold the current president and Congress to the same accounting standards to which we hold the private sector? For example, see if you can find out how often

corporate CEOs are replaced compared to the frequency with which U.S. presidents are replaced. Similarly, try to learn how often boards of directors change membership, compared to Congress. If turnover is higher in one sector than in another, would this imply that budget projections would be systematically more optimistic in that sector, or just more likely to be wrong one way or the other?

# FOUR

# Monetary Policy and Financial Institutions

# 18

# *The Future of the Fed: New Economy versus Inflation Targeting*

Some have said that the chair of the **Federal Reserve System (the Fed)** is the most powerful policymaker not only in the United States, but also in the world. This is quite a burden to bear, although successful chairs often serve for many years. Alan Greenspan, for example, has presided over America's central bank for more than a decade and a half. During much of his tenure, the U.S. economy was blessed with low unemployment, low inflation, and relatively strong economic growth.

## The Fed and the New Economy

Some have called Greenspan the quintessential new economist because he understood the **new economy**—one based on a dramatic growth in information technology that created even faster **productivity** growth. This rapid rise in productivity in the 1990s allowed the economy to grow rapidly without much inflation. During the 1990s, Greenspan's claim to fame was that he allowed the **money supply** to grow rapidly in the face of naysayers who argued that such rapid monetary growth would lead to increasing rates of inflation. In retrospect, his monetary policy prescription for the 1990s turned out to be correct. He presided over a period in which Americans experienced higher **real wages,** a soaring stock market, and increasing amounts of **business investment.**

## Enter the 2000s—A Changed Economic Landscape

According to an old saying, what goes up must come down. Although this does not always apply in economic matters, it turns out that this is precisely what happened with major parts of the economy in the early 2000s. After the technology boom ended quite abruptly in 2000 and 2001, the stock market fell dramatically in value, and the economy quickly slid into **recession.** The recession turned out to be both mild and brief by historical standards, but Greenspan's critics blamed the stock market meltdown on him. They also argued that the Fed was facing not inflation, but **deflation** (see Chapter 9). During the early 2000s, the Fed utilized expansionary monetary policy, as evidenced by its adjusting downward "the" interest rate on a regular basis (see Chapter 19).

As the mid-2000s rolled around, the Fed's critics argued that the chair of the Fed had run out of policy options and that the future of the Fed was in doubt. Most notably, Fed critics claimed that the economy will always transform itself in response to changes in regulation and technology. As a result of this ever-evolving economic structure, monetary guidelines used at one moment may not work in an apparently similar situation during another period. So, although what Greenspan did was right in the 1990s, the same policy may not work again, even under seemingly duplicate nationwide conditions.

By the time you read this, the Fed may have a new chair, or perhaps Greenspan will stay on. What can we expect future monetary policy to look like?

## Is Inflation Targeting in the Fed's Future?

Certainly, we will not expect to see anytime soon our central bank operating according to a **monetary rule,** which would involve setting and adhering to a target rate of growth for the money supply. Instead, the Fed's future may lie in a relatively simple concept—**inflation targeting.** The central bank of New Zealand has already successfully used this policy formula.

Most central banks (including the Fed) see themselves as having many jobs—juggling unemployment, inflation, the balance of payments, and so forth. A few years back, however, the government in New Zealand decided to give its central bank just one job: keeping the price level stable—the extreme form of inflation targeting. In 1989, New Zealand passed its Reserve Bank Act, which set the desired rate of inflation at 0 to 2 percent. In essence, there is a contract between the government and central bank officials who are directly responsible for price stability. If the Reserve Bank of New Zealand, that nation's central bank, fails to achieve this single goal, its chair can be fired. To fulfill its mandate, the Reserve Bank of New Zealand ignores variations in short-run real (or nominal) GDP growth rates. It focuses only on inflation.

At least initially, the central bank's increased independence and explicit mission appear to have worked. When the Reserve Bank Act was passed in 1989, the annual rate of inflation in New Zealand was 5.7 percent, as measured by changes in the consumer price index. Currently, the rate of inflation in New Zealand is running at about 1.5 percent per year.

Many long-time critics of the U.S. central bank claim that its ultimate goal should be only to control inflation, just as in New Zealand. Why? These critics say that in the long run the Fed simply cannot control real economic growth or productivity. Rather, it can control only one variable—the rate of inflation.

A Federal Reserve policy of inflation targeting would mean that the chair of the Fed would set a target range for inflation both *publicly* and regularly. The chair would then report to Congress on how well the Fed had met its goal, similar to what happens in New Zealand. The purported advantage of this type of monetary policy is that it reduces uncertainty. If the Fed set a target of, say, 2.5 percent for the rate of inflation, economic agents—consumers and businesspersons—would know that when the inflation rate rose above that level, the Fed would start tightening monetary policy by cutting monetary growth. If the inflation rate fell below 2.5 percent, economic agents would know that the Fed would increase the rate of growth of the money supply.

## An Opposing View—"Anti-Bubble" Policy

Yet another group of Fed critics argues *against* inflation targeting. These critics believe that Greenspan was responsible for the stock market **bubble** in the 1990s. They claim that the Fed chair allowed the stock market bubble to distort the economy. When the stock market started taking off in 1996, they say, the Fed should have set higher interest rates to dampen the "irrational exuberance" of the period.

These economists support an "anti-bubble" monetary policy because they believe that financial bubbles lead to economic instability. They are worried that when financial bubbles pop, deflationary forces become too strong.

So how would this alternative monetary policy work? An anti-bubble policy is a little harder to explain—and to put into action—than inflation targeting. In principle, the Fed would create policies that act against the current tide of economic affairs, in this case against excessive increases in any important **asset market** prices. If a housing bubble was getting out of hand, for example—housing prices, on average, rising substantially faster than the general rate of inflation—then Fed policy should be restrictive. If the U.S. stock market started rapidly rising in value relative to its long-run average, this bubble would also trigger contractionary monetary policy.

## There Are Problems with Both Policy Prescriptions

The chair of the Fed has routinely resisted a policy of publicly announced inflation targeting. Greenspan, for example, has constantly pointed out that the economy changes. He therefore argues that the appropriate inflation goal is not the same over time. He has also argued that explicit inflation targeting would unduly restrict the Fed chair in the event of crises, such as the stock market crash in October 1987 and the terrorist attacks on September 11, 2001. During such crises, inflation targeting would have tied the Fed chair's hands at a time when the Fed needed to restore public confidence. The same would be true in the future.

As for the proposed "anti-bubble" policy, many argue that it is impossible to know when a rise in asset prices actually represents a "bubble"—which is to say, a rise greater than it "should" be. Under an anti-bubble mandate, the Fed would have to second-guess financial markets. An anti-bubble policy could also stifle, or at least reduce, economic growth. Historically, the Fed has not done too well when it broadened its policy making to include looking at the stock market. In the 1920s, for example, the chair of the Fed, Adolph Miller, instituted a concerted campaign to rein in the stock market bubble. The result: monetary policy was severely restricted in 1928 and 1929 even though inflation was practically zero. In October 1929, the stock market suffered its most severe crash in modern times. So far, none of the anti-bubble advocates have come up with a way to ensure that similar mistakes by the Fed would not occur—with similar disastrous consequences.

So our bet, then, is simple: no matter who the chair of the Fed may be, neither the anti-inflation advocates nor the anti-bubble advocates will have their way completely. But, because both inflation and asset bubbles entail high potential costs, you can be equally sure that both camps will have a role in shaping whatever policy does emerge.

## For Critical Analysis

1. The Fed has never seriously considered using a monetary rule, which would entail forgetting about discretionary monetary policy. Why would you predict that the Board of Governors of the Federal Reserve System would be emphatically against a monetary rule?

2. Under which possible policy—inflation targeting or anti-bubble—would the chair of the Fed have more discretionary power? Why?

3. Why is there no discussion of the possibility that the Fed might follow an "unemployment targeting" policy or a "real economic growth targeting" policy? (Hint: Can the Fed change the unemployment rate or the rate of growth of real income with its policy tools?)

# 19

# *Monetary Policy and Interest Rates*

"The Fed lowers interest rates by one-half point." That and similar headlines appeared numerous times in the financial press during the early 2000s. The Fed—short for the **Federal Reserve System**—is America's **central bank.** Interest rates can be affected by the Fed; when they are, that is part of **monetary policy,** defined as the use of changes in the amount of money in circulation to affect interest rates, credit markets, inflation, and unemployment.

The theory behind monetary policy is relatively simple. An increase in the money supply raises spending on goods and services and, thus, stimulates the economy, tending to lower unemployment in the short run and raise inflation in the long run. (One important version of the **money supply** is composed of checking-type account balances and currency in the hands of the public.) The flip side is that a decrease in the money supply reduces spending, thereby depressing the economy; the short-run result is higher unemployment, and the long-run effect is a lower inflation rate.

## Monetary Policy and the Fed

Congress established the Federal Reserve System in 1913. A Board of Governors consisting of seven members, including the very powerful chairperson, governs it. All of the governors, including the chair, are nominated by the president and approved by the Senate. Their appointments are for fourteen years (although the chair serves in that role for only four years at a time).

Through the Fed, and its Federal Open Market Committee (FOMC), decisions about monetary policy are made eight times a year. The Federal Reserve System is independent; the Board even has its own budget, financed with interest earnings on the portfolio of bonds it owns. The president can attempt to persuade the Board to follow a particular policy, and Congress can threaten to merge the Fed with the Treasury or otherwise restrict its behavior. But unless Congress takes the radical step of passing legislation to the contrary, the Fed's chair and governors can do what they please. Hence, talking about "the president's monetary policy" or "Congress's monetary policy" is inaccurate. To be sure, the Fed has, on occasion, yielded to presidential pressure to pursue a particular policy, and the Fed's chair follows a congressional resolution directing him to report on what the Fed is doing on the policy front. But now, more than ever before, the Fed remains the single most important and truly independent source of economic power in the federal government. Monetary policy is Fed policy and no one else's.

Federal Reserve monetary policy, in principle, is supposed to be counter-cyclical. That is, it is supposed to counteract other forces that might be making the economy contract or expand too rapidly. The economy goes through so-called **business cycles,** made up of recessions (and sometimes depressions), when unemployment is rising, and expansions, when unemployment is falling and businesses often are straining their productive capacity. For the Fed to stabilize the economy, it must create policies that go counter to business activity. Although Fed policy can be put into place much faster than most federal policies, it still does not operate instantaneously. Indeed, researchers have estimated that it takes almost fourteen months for a change in monetary policy to become effective. Thus, by the time monetary policy goes into effect, a different policy might be appropriate.

## Policy in Practice

Researchers examining the evidence over the period from 1913 until the 1990s have concluded that, on average, the Fed's policy has turned out to be pro-cyclical, rather than counter-cyclical. That is, by the time the Fed started pumping money into the economy, it was time to do the opposite; and by the time the Fed started reducing the growth rate of the money supply, it was time to start increasing it. Perhaps the Fed's biggest pro-cyclical blunder occurred during the Great Depression in the 1930s. Many economists believe that what would have been a severe recession turned into the Great Depression because the Fed's actions resulted in an almost one-third decrease in the amount of money in circulation, drastically reducing aggregate spending. It has also been argued that the rapid inflation experienced in the 1970s was largely the result of excessive monetary expansion by the Fed.

In the 1990s, few commentators were able to complain about monetary policy. Inflation almost disappeared by the end of the decade, which also saw the unemployment rate drop to its lowest level in nearly forty years. Why the Fed was successful in the 1990s remains unclear. It could have been due to the uniquely superior insights of its chair, Alan Greenspan. Or perhaps the Fed had learned from its past experiences. Or it simply may have been a run of good luck. But whatever the reason, it is clear that the Fed remains far from perfect. Late in the decade, it tightened monetary policy sharply, reducing monetary growth and thereby contributing to the recession of 2001. Moreover, some economists are worried that the Fed may have increased the growth rate of the money supply too much in 2001 and 2002 to counter that recession. If they are correct, this means that the Fed will have set the stage for renewed inflation later. Indeed, by 2004, the Fed itself was worried about just that possibility. This led it to change its policy to a more restrictive stance, resulting in headlines that read, "Fed raises interest rates by one-quarter point."

## Inflation and Interest Rates

Most newspaper discussions of Fed policy focus on its decisions to raise or lower interest rates. Before we can make any sense out of such discussions, first we need to understand the relationship between **nominal interest rates,** that is, the rates that you see in the newspaper and pay for loans, and the **expected rate of inflation.**

Let's start in a hypothetical world where there is no inflation, so expected (or anticipated) inflation is zero. In that world, you might be able to borrow—obtain a mortgage to buy a home, for example—at a nominal rate of interest of, say, 4 percent. If you borrow the funds and your anticipation of zero inflation turns out to be accurate, neither you nor the lender will have been fooled. The dollars you pay back in the years to come will be just as valuable in terms of purchasing power as the dollars that you borrowed. In this situation, we would say that the **real rate of interest** (equal to the nominal rate of interest minus the anticipated rate of inflation) was exactly equal to the nominal interest rate.

Contrast this with a situation in which the expected inflation rate is, say, 5 percent. Although you would be delighted to borrow at a 4 percent interest rate, lenders would be reluctant to oblige you, and their reluctance would be based on exactly the same reasoning you would be using: the dollars with which you would be repaying the debt would be declining in purchasing power every year of the debt. Lenders would likely insist upon (and you would agree to) an **inflationary premium** of 5 percent, to make up for the expected inflation. Hence, the nominal interest rate would rise to about 9 percent, keeping the real rate at its previous level of 4 percent.

There is strong evidence that inflation rates and nominal interest rates move in parallel. During periods of rapid inflation, people come to anticipate that inflation rather promptly, and higher nominal interest rates are the result. In the early 1970s, when the inflation rate was between 4 and 5 percent, nominal interest rates on mortgages were around 8 to 10 percent. At the beginning of the 1980s, when the inflation rate was near 10 percent, nominal interest rates on mortgages had risen to between 14 and 16 percent. By the middle of the 1990s, when the inflation rate was 2 to 3 percent, nominal interest rates had fallen to between 6 and 8 percent.

## Policy and Interest Rates

Now let's go back to Fed policy and the headlines. When the chair of the Fed states that the Fed is raising "the" interest rate from, say, 1.25 percent to 1.5 percent, he really means something else. In the first place, the interest rate referred to is the **federal funds rate,** or the rate at which banks can borrow excess reserves from other banks. Any effects of Fed policy here will show up in other rates only indirectly. More importantly, even when the Fed decides to try to alter the federal funds rate, it can do so only by actively entering the market for federal government securities (usually Treasury bills). So, if the Fed wants to lower "the" interest rate as it did in the early 2000s, it essentially must buy Treasury bills from banks and other private holders of the bills. This action bids up the prices of these bills and simultaneously lowers the interest rates on them. This, in turn, lowers the interest rates at which banks are willing to lend to each other and to the public. (In terms of our earlier discussion, this policy also has the effect of increasing the money supply and so increases spending throughout the economy.) Conversely, when the Fed wants to increase "the" rate of interest as in the mid-2000s, it *sells* Treasury bills, driving their prices down and pushing up interest rates. The result is a reduction in the money supply and a reduction in spending throughout the economy. The pre-announcement of the policy change, which comes in the form of a Fed declaration that interest rates are going to be changed, simply serves to alert people that a new policy is on the way.

The other key point to note is that the changes in interest rates we have been talking about are very much short-term changes—and are occurring over a period of time short enough that the expected inflation rate is constant. Once the effects of the Fed's new policy begin to kick in, however, the expected inflation rate will tend to respond, which can create a whole new set of problems. For example, suppose the Fed decides to "lower interest rates," that is, to increase the money supply by buying Treasury bills. In the early weeks and months, this will indeed lower interest rates and stimulate spending. But, for a given level of productive capacity in the economy, this added spending will eventually be translated into a higher inflation rate. This will soon cause nominal interest rates to *rise,* as inflationary expectations get added onto the real interest rate.

The fact of the matter is that although the Fed can cause interest rates to move up or down in the short run via its choice of monetary policy, forces beyond its control determine what interest rates will be in the long run. The real rate is determined by the underlying productivity of the economy and the consumption preferences of individuals, and the expected inflation rate is determined by people's beliefs about future policy. Thus, when you read that the chair of the Fed has raised "the" interest rate, you know that the growth of the money supply has been reduced. But you also now know that whether the Fed likes it or not, if this policy persists long enough, the eventual result will be less inflation in the future and thus lower, not higher, interest rates.

## For Critical Analysis

1. Why do you suppose the Fed likes to signal its intentions about monetary policy ahead of time?
2. Some economists have argued that the Fed should stick to a simple "monetary rule," such as a stable growth rate of the money supply, regardless of what is going on in the economy.

Given the Fed's performance history, can you suggest why we might benefit from such a rule? Why do you think the Fed has steadfastly refused to implement such a rule?

3. One effect of the September 11, 2001 terrorist attacks was to temporarily prevent banks from accessing reserves they needed to meet the demands of their customers. (This occurred because the attacks destroyed many records as well as the computers required to access backup records, and it took affected banks several weeks to become fully operational.) In response, the Fed made many billions of dollars of reserves available to banks, gradually withdrawing the new reserves from the banking system as that system returned to normality. Suppose the Fed had not injected reserves in this way. What would likely have happened to interest rates as a result? What would have been the likely impact on the stock market and on spending by consumers and businesses? Would the unemployment rate have gone up or down?

# 20

# *Beating the Market*

There is no doubt that a knowledge of macroeconomics can help you understand many important economic factors, including the determinants of the unemployment rate and the inflation rate, and what causes changes in interest rates and the prices of the stocks issued by corporations. But sometimes people think that this level of understanding can take them a step further and enable them to forecast *ahead of time* what the behavior of key macroeconomic variables is likely to be in the future. Now, when it comes to forecasting the unemployment rate, the inflation rate, or even the level of real GDP, the principles of macroeconomics definitely can help. But when it comes to the stock market or to interest rates, we want to emphatically (albeit sadly) inform you of this: nothing you learn from this (or any other) book will enable you to "beat the market" by figuring out ahead of everyone else where stock prices, bond prices, or interest rates are going to be tomorrow or next year.

## Stocks, Bonds, and Brokers

Let's begin with the financial pages (sometimes called the business section) of the daily newspaper. There you will find column after column of information about the stocks and bonds of U.S. corporations. **A share of stock** in a corporation is simply a legal claim to a share of the corporation's future profits; owners of stocks are called **shareholders.** Thus, if there are 100,000 shares of stock in a company and you, as a shareholder, own 1,000 of them, then you own the right to 1 percent of that company's future profits.

A **bond** is a legal claim against a firm, entitling the bond owner to receive a fixed annual "coupon" payment, plus a lump sum payment at the bond's maturity date. (Coupon payments on bonds get their name from the fact that bonds once had coupons attached to them when issued. Each year, the owner would clip a coupon off the bond and send it to the issuing firm in return for that year's interest payment.) Bonds are issued in return for funds lent to the firm. The coupon payments represent interest on the amount borrowed by the firm, and the lump sum payment at maturity generally equals the amount originally borrowed. Bonds are *not* claims to the future profits of the firm; legally, the owners of the bonds, called **bondholders,** are to be paid whether the firm prospers or not. (To ensure this, bondholders generally must receive their coupon payments each year, plus any principal due, before *any* shareholders can receive their share of the firm's profits, called **dividends.**)

Now, suppose that in your quest for riches, you decide to buy some shares of stock in a corporation. How should you choose which corporation's stock to buy? One way is to consult a specialist in stocks, called a **stockbroker.** Such brokers have access to an enormous amount of information. They can tell you what lines of business specific corporations are in, who the firms' major competitors are, how profitable the firms have been in the past, and whether their stocks' prices have risen or fallen. If pressed, they probably will be willing to recommend which stocks to buy. Throughout, any broker's opinion will sound highly informed and authoritative.

Strange as it may seem, though, a broker's investment advice is not likely to be any better than anyone else's. In fact, *the chances of the broker being right are no greater than the chances of you being right!* On average you are just as likely to get rich by throwing darts at the financial pages of your newspaper. Let's see why.

## The Magic of the Darts

Some years ago, the editors of *Forbes,* a respected business magazine, taped the financial pages of a major newspaper to a wall and threw darts at the portion listing stock prices. They hit the stocks of twenty-eight different companies and invested a hypothetical $1,000 in each. When the editors halted their experiment, the original $28,000 had grown to $132,000—a gain of 370 percent. Over the same period, the Dow Jones Industrial Average (a leading measure of the stock market's overall performance) grew less than 40 percent in value. Perhaps even more impressive, *Forbes'* random selection of stocks outperformed the recommended stock portfolios of most of the stock market forecasting "gurus."

More recently, the editors of *The Wall Street Journal,* a major financial newspaper, tried a similar experiment. Each month they invited four stockbrokers to recommend a stock to buy; the four stocks became the "experts' portfolio" for the month. Then, the editors threw four darts at the financial pages of their newspaper to select four stocks that became the "darts' portfolio" for the month. Over time, the particular expert brokers changed, depending on how well their picks performed relative to the darts' portfolio. Any broker whose stock beat the darts got to pick again the next month. Any expert beaten by the darts was replaced the next month by a new broker. At six month intervals, the newspaper tallied up the performances of the experts versus the darts. After several years of running the experiment, the general result was this:  Although the experts beat the darts over the long haul, the winning margin was tiny.  Moreover, there were several six-month periods in which the darts actually *outperformed* the experts. How did the darts do it?

## Buy Low, Sell High

Suppose that you, and you alone, noticed that the price of a particular stock moved in a predictable manner. Specifically, assume the price *rose* 5 percent on even-numbered days and *fell* 5 percent on odd-numbered days, resulting in (approximately) no average change over time. Knowing this fact, how do you make money? You simply buy shares of the stock just before their price is due to rise, and sell shares of the stock just before it is due to fall. If you start the year with $1,000 and reinvest your profits, following this strategy would yield profits in excess of $500,000 by the end of the year. If you successfully continue this strategy for a second year, your wealth would exceed $250 million!

Of course, as your wealth accumulates—"buying low and selling high"—your purchases and sales would start to affect the price of the stock. In particular, your purchases would drive up the low prices and your sales would drive down the high prices. Ultimately, your buying and selling in response to predictable patterns would *eliminate* those patterns, and there would be no profit potential left to exploit. This is *exactly* what happens in the stock market—except it happens far faster than a single person could accomplish it alone.

## A Random Walk Down Wall Street

At any point in time, there are tens of thousands, perhaps millions, of people looking for any bit of information that will help them forecast the future prices of stocks. Responding to any information that seems useful, these people try to "buy low and sell high," just as you would like to do. As a result, all publicly available information that might be used to forecast stock prices gets taken into account—leaving no predictable profits. Plus, because there are so many people involved in this process, it occurs quite swiftly. Indeed, there is evidence that all information entering the market is fully incorporated into stock prices within *less than a minute* of its arrival.

The result is that stock prices tend to follow a **random walk**—which is to say that the best forecast of tomorrow's price is today's price, plus a random component. Although large values of the random component are less likely than small values, nothing else about its magnitude or sign (positive or negative) can be predicted. Indeed, the random component of stock prices exhibits behavior much like what would occur if you rolled two dice and subtracted seven from the resulting score. *On average,* the dice will total 7, so after you subtract 7, the average result will be zero. It is true that rolling a 12 or a 2 (yielding a net score of +5 or −5) is less likely than rolling an 8 or a 6 (producing a net score of +1 or −1). Nevertheless, positive and negative net scores are equally likely, and the expected net score is zero.[1]

It is worth emphasizing that the bond market operates every bit as efficiently as the stock market. That is, investors in bonds study the available information and use whatever might help them forecast future bond prices. Because they exploit this information up to the point that the benefits of doing so are just matched by the costs, there remains no publicly available information that can be used profitably to improve bond price forecasts. As a result, bond prices, like stock prices, follow a random walk. Moreover, because interest rates are inextricably linked to the prices of bonds, interest rates also follow a random walk.

## What Are Those People Doing?

In light of this discussion, two questions arise. First, are all the efforts put into forecasting stock and bond prices simply a waste? The answer is no. From a social viewpoint, this effort is productive because it helps ensure that asset prices correctly reflect all available information, and, thus, that resources are allocated efficiently. From a private standpoint, the effort is also rewarding, just as any other productive activity is rewarding. At

---

[1]Strictly speaking, stock prices follow a random walk with **drift;** that is, on average they rise at a real (inflation-adjusted) rate of about 3 percent per year over long periods of time. This drift, which is the average compensation investors receive for deferring consumption, can be thought of as the seven that comes up on average when two dice are rolled.

the margin, the gains from trying to forecast future stock and bond prices are exactly equal to the costs; there are no unexploited profit opportunities. Unless you happen to have some unique ability that makes you better than others, you will earn only enough to cover your costs—but, of course, the same is true of growing wheat or selling women's shoes. So, absent some special ability, you are just as well-off investing in the market based on the roll of the dice or the throw of a dart.

The second question is a bit trickier: Isn't there any way to "beat the market"? The answer is yes—but only if you have **inside information,** i.e., information unavailable to the public. Suppose, for example, that your best friend is in charge of new product development for Mousetrap Inc., a firm that just last night invented a mousetrap superior to all others on the market. No one but your friend—and now you—are aware of this. You could indeed make money with this information, by purchasing shares of Mousetrap Inc. and then selling them (at a higher price) as soon as the invention is publicly announced. There is one problem: stock trading based on such inside information is illegal, punishable by substantial fines and even imprisonment. Unless you happen to have a stronger-than-average desire for a long vacation in a federal prison, our money-making advice to you is simple: invest in the mousetrap after it hits the market—and throw darts in the meantime.

## For Critical Analysis

1. Why do you think the government prohibits insider trading?
2. When the prices of stocks fall, newspapers often report that the decline in prices was caused by a "wave of selling." By the definition of exchange, every sale must be accompanied by a purchase. Why, then, do the newspapers not report that the decline in stock prices was caused by a "wave of purchasing"?
3. If stockbrokers cannot "beat the market", why do people use their services?

# *The Case against Cash*

There is a saying that, during bad economic times, "cash is king." This saying comes from the fact that those who hold cash (1) don't have to worry about falling stock prices and (2) are in a position to pounce on "good deals," meaning investment opportunities that can be had for a song if one has cash to pay for them.

From a purely economic point of view, the term *cash* in the above paragraph simply means any liquid assets that can be quickly and cheaply converted into other assets. But what about *real* cash, that is to say, **currency?** The statement "cash is king" usually has a different meaning when applied to currency. In this context, the royal status of cash comes from its suitability in laundering illegally obtained gains from drug trafficking and tax evasion. First, let's examine why currency is used so much in such activities.

## How to Cash In When What You Are Doing Is Illegal

Drug traffickers don't want to leave any trace of their illegal business activities. Consequently, you won't find many drug traffickers accepting checks or credit cards in exchange for the illicit goods they are selling. So, drug traffickers end up with huge amounts of currency. Then, they are faced with a problem: How to protect this currency and how to spend it without sending signals to drug agents and others that they are living "beyond their means."

There are two possibilities for the drug traffickers. They can attempt to transfer money out of the United States, for example, to other countries where officials and bankers are less concerned about the origins of such money. Alternatively, they can attempt to launder this currency. **Money laundering** is relatively straightforward. A legitimate business is formed, usually with a legitimate partner. This business has to be one that takes in large amounts of currency, such as a dry-cleaning establishment, a bar, or a restaurant. Little by little, the currency-laden drug dealer injects more and more of her or his cash into the business. The business shows an increasing profit, and the drug dealer is a seemingly legitimate partner in that business. She or he can then declare the increasing income on her or his tax returns. In that way, the lifestyle of the drug dealer will not be too far out of line with her or his actual declared income.

For many years, the federal government has attempted to thwart such behavior by requiring depository institutions to file a report whenever anyone deposits, withdraws, or transfers abroad more than $10,000 in U.S. funds. Apparently, though, many depository institutions have been unable or unwilling to turn away profitable activities with somewhat less-than-upstanding citizens and have consequently skirted this law. Indeed, some observers estimate that illegally obtained gains from drug deals account for at least $500 billion of money transfers throughout the world each year. So much for making it difficult for drug dealers to deal in cash.

## Enter the U.S.A. Patriot Act

After the terrorist attacks on September 11, 2001, the federal government discovered that terrorist activities were being funded by numerous organizations throughout the world that claimed to be charities. (Some of them may have actually performed as charities, but they apparently funded terrorists, too.) The government also discovered that certain rich individuals were using the banking system to finance terrorist activities. In response, President George W. Bush signed Title III of the U.S.A. Patriot Act on October 26, 2001, in an attempt to reduce the flow of funds to terrorist organizations.

One of the main aspects of this legislation is the requirement that all financial institutions use anti-money-laundering (AML) controls. Not surprisingly, sales of AML computer software programs have skyrocketed. In 2002 alone, U.S. banks spent over $60 million on AML technology. Globally, AML technology expenditures exceeded $200 million in that same year. Sophisticated AML software had to be developed because humans simply are not able to analyze a typical bank's thirty million transactions a year and identify all of the suspect transactions. Therefore, they may unwittingly launder funds for drug dealers or terrorists.

AML technology analyzes transactions at a bank and recognizes suspicious patterns of activity. It also looks for the names of "blacklisted" individuals and corporations with which it can match transactions. Further, it immediately spots certain types of transactions, such as those over a certain amount. Think of AML technology as a mass cross-referencing software system. The U.S.A. Patriot Act is forcing banks to bring all their transactional data through one single point. That allows them in a single view to look at all transactions and to know more about what their clients are doing—especially the possibly unsavory kind.

What can we predict about the future use of currency in light of this technology? Simply that drug dealers, tax cheats, and terrorists are going to have a harder time moving their cash around the world. Certainly, the end of cash is not near, but its use will not be as easy or as undocumented as it has been in the past.

## Moving toward Electronic Transactions by All

Increasingly, the Internet is becoming a part of our financial system. Remember that the full definition of money includes currency plus checking-type deposits. In the age of the Internet, it has seemed a little strange that the U.S. financial system still uses trucks and airplanes to move boxes of paper checks from bank to bank. That is starting to change.

The number of checks written annually peaked in the late 1990s and has been falling steadily ever since. At the same time, the use of credit and debit cards has risen from 18 percent to about a third of all forms of payment. Debit and credit card transactions are an increasingly attractive way to conduct business. All you receive are statements; there are no canceled checks to hold; and everything consists of magnetic impulses or other types of records on electronic storage devices.

Little by little, Americans are getting used to receiving certain payments, such as Social Security benefits and tax refunds, through electronic transfer into their bank accounts without depositing a check. Little by little, certain bills are being paid electronically, meaning that customers' checking accounts are simply debited for those bills, such as electricity and telephone service. These debits are turned into credits in the bank accounts of the selling companies.

As the United States moves from a paper-check-and currency-oriented society to an **electronic payments system,** the actual use of currency and checks will continue to fall. This decline in cash use will accelerate as true **e-cash** becomes more popular. E-cash is simply cash balances embedded in smart cards and computer hard drives that individuals eventually will be able to use, particularly for payment for small items in retail outlets such as drug stores and gas stations and on the Internet. While the use of e-cash has not yet caught on in the United States, its future looks promising. After all, wouldn't it be nice to carry something no bigger than a credit card instead of a wad of bills and a lump of coins?

So, the bottom line is that the reign of cash seems to be nearing its end, at least as the term *cash* has long been understood. Currency is losing its usefulness in drug deals and terrorist activities because it is now easier to track, and currency and checks are slowly becoming e-cash and digital records, rather than paper and metallic objects. The next question probably will be: Where will we put all those portraits of dead presidents?

## For Critical Analysis

1. Will drug traffickers be better or worse off as a result of the trend toward increased debit and credit card use as well as increased automated electronic deposits and withdrawals?
2. Those who avoid taxes often do so by getting paid in cash. Is there an effective way to reduce such tax evasion?
3. It is estimated that much of the currency that is counted as being part of the money supply of the United States is actually located in foreign nations, being used to lubricate terrorist activities and illegal drug deals. (The favorite denomination for such activities is the $100 bill, featuring Benjamin Franklin on its front.) How does the widespread use of U.S. currency in foreign lands complicate the policy choices of the Federal Reserve System?

# 22

# *Don't Worry, Your Deposits Are Insured*

Imagine hearing an unpleasant rumor about the commercial bank, savings and loan, or credit union in which you have a checking or savings account. Specifically, suppose the rumor was that your **depository institution** was on shaky financial grounds and that there was a significant chance that the institution would go under. Would you immediately rush to the bank to protect your funds by withdrawing them? Almost surely, the answer is "no." Why not? Because an agency of the federal government insures most deposits of banks and similar institutions, up to $100,000 for each deposit. So, it matters little to you as a depositor whether your bank goes under, because you know that Uncle Sam will bail you out. You might say, then, that for deposits up to $100,000 in any insured depository institution in the United States, you have a *zero* risk of losing your money. This was not always the case.

## When There Were "Runs" on Banks

A **bank run** is a simultaneous rush of depositors to convert their deposits into currency. Until the federal government set up deposit insurance in 1933, runs on banks were infrequent but seemingly unavoidable occurrences, sometimes becoming widespread during economic **recessions.** The largest number of bank runs in modern history occurred during the Great Depression, when bank failures averaged 2,000 each year during a several-year period.

Put yourself in the shoes of a depositor in a typical bank in 1930, and remember that you are a **creditor** of the bank. That is to say, your deposits in the bank are its **liabilities.** Suppose you hear a rumor that the **assets** of the bank are not sufficient to cover its liabilities. In other words, the bank is, or will soon be, **insolvent.** Presumably, you are worried that you won't get your deposits back in the form of currency. Knowing this, you are likely to rush to the bank. All other depositors who hear about the bank's supposedly weak financial condition are likely to do the same thing.

This is the essence of a bank run: regardless of the true state of a bank's financial condition, rumors or fears that the bank is in trouble can cause depositors to suddenly attempt to withdraw all of their funds. But many bank assets typically are in the form of loans that cannot immediately be converted into cash. Even if the bank is solvent, it is said to be **illiquid** because it doesn't have enough cash on hand to meet the demands of fearful depositors. And, when it attempts to get that cash by selling some assets, any resulting decline in the market value of those assets can quickly turn a **solvent** bank into an insolvent one. There are many famous old black-and-white pictures of hordes of depositors trying to get into banks during the Great Depression in order to withdraw their deposits in the form of currency.

## Enter Deposit Insurance

When bank failures reached their maximum of over 4,000 in one year during the early 1930s, the federal government decided to act to prevent further bank runs. In 1933, Congress passed, and the president signed into law, legislation creating the Federal Deposit Insurance Corporation (FDIC); the next year the Federal Savings and Loan Insurance Corporation

(FSLIC) was created. Many years later, in 1971, the National Credit Union Share Insurance Fund (NCUSIF) was created to insure credit union deposits, and in 1989 the FSLIC was replaced with the Savings Association Insurance Fund (SAIF). To keep our discussion simple, we will focus only on the FDIC, but the general principles apply to all of these agencies.

When the FDIC was formed, it insured against loss each account in a commercial bank, up to $2,500. That number was gradually increased to its current level of $100,000. The result of creating federally backed deposit insurance is that there has not been a significant bank run in the United States since the Great Depression, although there have been numerous bank failures in the interim. While this all sounds well and good, the U.S. economy has paid a high price at times because of the unintended consequences of deposit insurance.

## The First Unintended Consequence of Deposit Insurance

Suppose someone offers you what she claims is a great investment opportunity. She tells you that if you invest $50,000, you will make a very high rate of return, say, 20 percent per year, a return much higher than the 3 percent your funds are currently earning elsewhere. No matter how much you trusted the person offering you this deal, you would probably do some serious investigation of the proposed investment before you handed over your hard-earned $50,000. You, like other people, would make a serious effort to determine the risk factors involved in this potential opportunity.

For example, if you use part of your savings to buy a house, you will undoubtedly have the structural aspects of the house checked out by an inspector before you sign on the dotted line. Similarly, if you plan to purchase an expensive piece of art, you surely will have an independent expert verify that the artwork is authentic. Typically, you will do the same every time you put your accumulated savings into any potential investment: you will look before you leap.

Now ask yourself the following question: When is the last time you examined the lending activities of the depository institution at which you have your checking or savings account? That is, when is the last time you worried about the financial condition of your local bank? We predict that the answer is "never." Indeed, why should you investigate? With federal deposit insurance, you know that, even if the depository institution that has your funds is taking big risks, you are personally risking nothing. If that depository institution fails, the federal government will—with a 100 percent certainty—make sure that you get 100 percent of your deposits back.

So, here we have it—the first unintended consequence of deposit insurance. Depositors like you no longer have any substantial incentive to investigate the risks of the loans that depository institutions are making. You care little about what the managers of your bank do with the deposits that you give them, because at worst you may suffer some minor inconvenience if your bank fails. So, unlike in the days before deposit insurance, the marketplace today does little to monitor or punish bad management at depository institutions.

## The Second Unintended Consequence of Deposit Insurance

Now let's look at bank managers' incentives to act cautiously when making loans. Note, first, that the riskier the loan, the higher the interest rate that a bank can charge. For example, if a developing country with a blemished track record in paying back its debt wishes to borrow from a U.S. depository institution, that country will have to pay a much higher interest rate than will a less risky debtor.

When trying to decide which loan applicants should receive funds, bank managers must weigh the trade-off between risk and return. Poor credit risks offer high profits if they actually pay off their debts, but good credit risks are more likely to pay off their debts. The right choice means higher profits for the bank and likely higher salaries and promotions for the managers. The wrong choice means losses and perhaps insolvency for the bank and new, less desirable careers for the managers.

To understand how bank mangers' incentives are changed by deposit insurance, consider two separate scenarios. In the first scenario, the bank manager is told to take $50,000 of depositors' funds to Las Vegas. The rules of the game are that he can bet however he wants, and the bank will *share* the winnings *and losses* equally with the deposit holders whose funds he has in trust. In the second scenario, the same bank manager with the same funds is given a different set of rules. This time the bank won't bear any of the losses, but it will share in any winnings from his bets in Las Vegas.

Under which set of rules do you think the bank manager will take the higher risks while betting in Las Vegas? Clearly, he will take higher risks in the second scenario because his bank will not suffer at all if he loses the entire $50,000. Yet, if he hits it big, say, by placing a successful bet on double-zero in roulette, his bank will share the profits, and he is likely to get a raise and a promotion.

Well, the second scenario is exactly the scenario facing the managers of federally insured depository institutions. If they make risky loans, thereby earning, at least in the short run, higher profits, they share in the "winnings." The result for them is higher salaries because their banks will be making higher profits. If some of these risky loans are not repaid, what is the likely outcome? The bank's losses are limited because the federal government (which is to say, you, the taxpayer) will cover any shortfall between the bank's assets and its liabilities. Thus, federal deposit insurance means that banks get to enjoy all of the profits of risk without bearing all of the consequences of that risk.

So, the second unintended consequence of deposit insurance is that bank managers have an incentive to take greater risks in their lending policies than they otherwise would. Indeed, when the economy turned down in the early 1980s, we got to see the consequences of exactly this change in incentives. From 1985 until the beginning of 1993, 1,065 commercial banks failed, at an average rate of more than ten times that for the preceding forty years. The losses from these failures totaled in the billions of dollars—paid for, of course, by you, the taxpayer.

## Paying for Deposit Insurance

For the first sixty years or so of federal deposit insurance, all depository institutions were charged modest fees for their insurance coverage. Unfortunately, the fee that a particular depository institution paid was completely unrelated to the riskiness of the loans it made. A bank that made loans to Ford Motor Company was charged the same rate for deposit insurance as a bank that made loans to a startup company with no track record whatsoever. Hence, not even the fees paid by banks for their insurance gave them any incentive to be prudent. This is completely unlike the private insurance markets, where high-risk customers are charged higher premiums, giving them at least some incentive to become low-risk customers.

In the early 1990s, the federal government made a feeble attempt to adjust fees for deposit insurance depending on the riskiness of a bank's lending activities. But the political strength of the depository institutions prevented any fundamental change in the system. To make matters worse, since the mid-1990s virtually all depository institutions have had to pay *nothing* for federal deposit insurance. Furthermore, some brokerage firms have figured out how to jump aboard the federal deposit insurance bandwagon. In the early 2000s, Salomon Smith Barney, Inc. and Merrill Lynch & Co. figured out a way to shift funds every night between clients' *uninsured* money market accounts and federally insured accounts at commercial banks owned by these two brokerage firms. Depositors who had placed funds (as much as $600,000) with those two firms were able to receive full deposit insurance coverage on them. The brokerage firms did not have to pay one penny to obtain this deposit insurance for their clients, even though taxpayers—which is to say, you—were subjected to additional financial risk.

The moral of this story is simple. When we say, "don't worry," that advice applies only to your bank, savings and loan, and credit union deposits. When it comes to your liabilities as a U.S. taxpayer, you have plenty to worry about.

## For Critical Analysis

1. If federal deposit insurance is provided to banks at no cost to them, who pays when an insured depository institution fails and its depositors are reimbursed for the full amount of their deposits?

2. In a world without deposit insurance, what are some of the mechanisms that would arise to "punish" bank managers who acted irresponsibly? (HINT: There are similar types of mechanisms for consumer goods and in the stock market.)

3. How does the existence of federal deposit insurance affect the ability of the Federal Reserve (the Fed) to control the money supply? (Hint: To answer, remember that in our banking system each dollar of reserves held by a bank can be used to support several dollars of deposits.) In particular, consider the possibility of a banking panic in the absence of federal deposit insurance, and address these queries:

    a. Suppose that depositors fear that their banks are (or soon will be) insolvent, and so attempt to convert their deposits into currency. What does this eventually do to the money supply?

    b. Similarly, suppose that banks worry that their depositors might begin to behave this way, and so the banks begin to build up excess reserves rather than using them to create new deposits by making loans. What impact does this have on the money supply?

    c. How could the Fed alter policy to counteract these developments?

# part FIVE

# International Trade and Finance

# 23

# *The Opposition to Free Trade*

The period since the early 1990s has been a time of great change on the international trade front. The North American Free Trade Agreement (NAFTA), for example, substantially reduced the barriers to trade among citizens of Canada, the United States, and Mexico. On a global scale, the Uruguay Round of the General Agreement on Tariffs and Trade (GATT) was ratified by 117 nations including the United States. Under the terms of this agreement, the World Trade Organization (WTO), whose membership now numbers more than 140, replaced GATT and **tariffs** were cut worldwide. Agricultural **subsidies** were also reduced, and patent protections were extended. Currently, the WTO is establishing a set of arbitration boards to settle international disputes over trade issues.

## The Gains from Trade

Many economists believe that both NAFTA and the agreements reached during the Uruguay Round were victories not only for free trade, but also for the citizens of the participating nations. Nevertheless, many noneconomists, particularly politicians, opposed these agreements, so it is important to understand what is beneficial about NAFTA, the Uruguay Round, the WTO, and free trade in general.

Voluntary trade creates new wealth. In voluntary trade, both parties in an exchange gain. They give up something of lesser value in return for something of greater value. In this sense, exchanges are always unequal. But it is this unequal nature of exchange that is the source of the increased **productivity** and higher wealth that occur whenever trade takes place. When we engage in exchange, what we give up is worth less than what we get—if this were not true, we would not have traded. What is true for us is also true for our trading partner, meaning that partner is better off, too. (Of course, sometimes *after* an exchange, you may believe that you were mistaken about the value of what you just received—this is called *buyer's remorse*, but it does not affect our discussion.)

Free trade encourages individuals to employ their talents and abilities in the most productive manner possible and to exchange the fruits of their efforts. The **gains from trade** arise from one of the fundamental ideas in economics—a nation gains from doing what it can do best *relative* to other nations, that is, by specializing in those endeavors in which it has a **comparative advantage.** Trade encourages individuals and nations to discover ways to specialize so that they can become more productive and enjoy higher incomes. Increased productivity and the subsequent increase in the rate of economic growth are exactly what the signatories of the Uruguay Round and NAFTA sought—and are obtaining—by reducing trade barriers.

## Keeping the Competition Out

Despite these gains from exchange, some (and sometimes many) people routinely oppose free trade, particularly in the case of international trade. This opposition comes in many guises, but they all basically come down to one. When our borders are open to trade with other nations, some individuals and businesses within our nation face more competition. Most firms and workers hate competition, and who can blame them? After all, if a firm can keep competitors out, its profits are sure to stay the same or even rise. And, if workers can prevent competition from other sources, they can enjoy higher wages and, perhaps, a larger selection of jobs. So, the real source of most opposition to international trade is that the opponents of trade dislike the competition that comes with it. This position is not immoral or unethical, but it is not altruistic or noble, either. It is based on self-interest, pure and simple.

Opposition to free trade is, of course, nothing new on the American landscape. In the last century, it resulted most famously in the Smoot-Hawley Tariff Act of 1930. This major federal statute was a classic example of **protectionism**—an effort to protect a subset of U.S. producers at the expense of consumers and other producers. It included tariff schedules for over 20,000 products, raising taxes on affected imports by an average of 52 percent.

The Smoot-Hawley Tariff Act encouraged "beggar-thy-neighbor" policies by the rest of the world. Such policies are an attempt to improve (a portion of) one's domestic economy at the expense of foreign countries' economies. In this case, tariffs were imposed to discourage imports in the hope that domestic import-competing industries would benefit. The United Kingdom, France, the Netherlands, and Switzerland soon adopted the beggar-thy-neighbor policy at the heart of the Smoot-Hawley Tariff Act. The result was a massive reduction in international trade. According to many economists, this caused a worldwide worsening of the Great Depression.

Opponents of free trade sometimes claim that beggar-thy-neighbor policies really do benefit the United States by protecting import-competing industries. In general, this claim is not correct. It is true that *some* Americans benefit from such policies, but two large groups of Americans *lose*. First, the purchasers of imports and import-competing goods suffer from the higher prices and reduced selection of goods and suppliers caused by tariffs and import **quotas.** Second, the decline in imports caused by protectionism also causes a decline in *exports,* thereby harming firms and workers in these industries. This result follows directly from one of the fundamental propositions in international trade:

*In the long run, imports are paid for by exports.*

This proposition simply states that when one country buys goods and services from the rest of the world (imports), the rest of the world eventually wants goods from that country (exports) in exchange. Given this fundamental proposition, a corollary becomes obvious:

*Any restriction on imports leads to a reduction in exports.*

Thus, any extra business for import-competing industries gained as a result of tariffs or quotas means at least as much business *lost* for exporting industries.

## The Arguments against Free Trade

Opponents to free trade often raise a variety of objections in their efforts to restrict it. For example, it is sometimes claimed that foreign companies engage in **dumping,** that is, selling their goods in the United States "below cost." The first question to ask when such charges are made is, Below *whose* cost? Clearly, if the foreign firm is selling in the United States, it must be offering the good for sale at a price that is at or below the costs of U.S. firms; otherwise it could not induce Americans to buy from it. But the ability of individuals or firms to obtain goods at lower cost is one of the *benefits* of free trade, not one of its damaging features.

What about claims that import sales are taking place at prices below the *foreign* company's costs? This amounts to arguing that the owners of the foreign company are voluntarily giving some of their wealth to us, namely, the difference between their costs and the (lower) price they charge us. It is possible, though unlikely, that they might wish to do this, perhaps because this could be the cheapest way of getting us to try a product that we would not otherwise purchase. But, even supposing it is true, why would we want to refuse this gift? As a nation, we are richer if we accept it. Moreover, it is a gift that will be offered only in the short run: there is no point in selling at prices below cost unless one hopes to soon raise the price profitably above cost!

Another argument sometimes raised against international trade is that the goods are produced abroad using "unfair" labor practices (such as the use of child labor) or production processes that do not meet U.S. environmental standards. Certainly, such charges are sometimes true. But we must remember two things here. First, although we may find the use of child labor (or perhaps 60-hour weeks with no overtime pay) objectionable, such practices were at one time commonplace in the United States. They were common in this country for the same reason they are currently practiced abroad: the people involved were (or are) too poor to do otherwise. Some families in developing nations literally cannot survive unless all family members contribute. As unfortunate as this situation is, if we insist on imposing our tastes—shaped in part by our extraordinarily high wealth—on peoples whose wealth is far lower than ours, we run the risk of making them worse off even as we think we are helping them.

Similar considerations apply to environmental standards. It is well-established that individuals' and nations' willingness to pay for environmental quality is very much shaped by their wealth. Environmental quality is a normal good; that is, people who are rich (such as Americans) want to consume more of it per capita than do people who are poor. Insisting that other nations meet environmental standards that we find acceptable is much like insisting that they wear the clothes we wear, use the modes of transportation we prefer, and consume the foods we like. The few people who can afford it will indeed be living in the style to which we are accustomed, but most people in developing countries will not be able to afford anything like that style.

There is one important exception to this argument. When foreign air or water pollution is generated near enough to our borders (for example, with Mexico or Canada) to cause harm to Americans, good public policy presumably dictates that we seek to treat that pollution as though it were being generated inside our borders.

Our point is not that foreign labor or environmental standards are, or should be, irrelevant to Americans. Instead, our point is that achieving high standards of either is costly, and trade restrictions are unlikely to be the most efficient or effective way to achieve them. Just as important, labor standards and environmental standards are all too often raised as smokescreens to hide the real motive: keeping the competition out.

## Why Are Antitrade Measures Passed?

If free trade is beneficial and restrictions on trade generally are harmful, we must surely ask, How does legislation such as the Smoot-Hawley Tariff Act (or any other trade restriction) ever get passed? The reason is that foreign competition often clearly affects a narrow and specific import-competing industry, such as textiles, shoes, or automobiles, and thus trade restrictions benefit a narrow, well-defined group of economic agents. For example, restrictions on imports of Japanese automobiles in the 1980s chiefly benefited the Big Three automakers in this country: General Motors, Ford, and Chrysler. Similarly, long-standing quotas on imports of sugar benefit a handful of large U.S. sugar producers. Because of the concentrated benefits that accrue when Congress votes in favor of trade restrictions, sufficient monies can be raised in those industries to aggressively lobby members of Congress to impose those restrictions.

The eventual reduction in exports that must follow is normally spread throughout all export industries. Thus, no specific group of workers, managers, or shareholders in export industries will feel that it should contribute money to lobby Congress to *reduce* international trade restrictions. Additionally, although consumers of imports and import-competing goods lose due to trade restrictions, they, too, are typically a diffuse group of individuals, none of whom individually will be affected a great deal because of any single import restriction.

This simultaneous existence of concentrated benefits and diffuse costs led Mark Twain to say many years ago that the free traders win the arguments but the protectionists win the votes.

Of course, the protectionists don't win *all* the votes—after all, about one-eighth of the U.S. economy is based on international trade. Despite the opposition to free trade that comes from many quarters, its benefits to the economy as a whole are so great that it is unthinkable that we might do away with international trade altogether. Both economic theory and empirical evidence clearly indicate that, on balance, Americans will be better off after—and because of—the move to freer trade through such developments as NAFTA and the WTO.

## For Critical Analysis

1. For a number of years, Japanese carmakers voluntarily limited the number of cars they exported to the United States. What effect do you think this had on Japanese imports of U.S. cars and U.S. exports of goods and services *other than* automobiles?
2. Until a few years ago, U.S. cars exported to Japan had the driver controls on the left side of the car (as in the United States). The Japanese, however, drive on the left side of the road, so Japanese cars sold in Japan have the driver controls on the right side. Suppose the Japanese tried to sell their cars in the United States with the driver controls on the right side. What impact would this likely have on their sales in this country? Do you think the unwillingness of U.S. carmakers to put the driver controls on the "correct" side for exports to Japan had any effect on their sales of cars in that country?
3. Keeping in mind the key propositions of international trade outlined in this chapter, what is the likely impact of international trade restrictions on the following variables in the United States: employment; the unemployment rate; real GDP; and the price level? Explain.

# 24

# *The $750,000 Job*

In even-numbered years, particularly years evenly divisible by four, politicians of all persuasions are apt to give long-winded speeches about the need to protect U.S. jobs from the evils of foreign competition. To accomplish this goal, we are encouraged to "Buy American." If further encouragement is needed, we are told that if we do not reduce voluntarily the amount of imported goods we purchase, the government will impose (or make more onerous) **tariffs** (taxes) on imported goods or **quotas** (quantity restrictions) that physically limit imports. The objective of this exercise is to "save" U.S. jobs.

Unlike African elephants or blue whales, U.S. jobs are in no danger of becoming extinct. There are virtually an unlimited number of potential jobs in the U.S. economy, and there always will be. Some of these jobs are not very pleasant, and many others do not pay very well, but there will always be employment of some sort as long as there is scarcity. Thus, when a steelworker making $72,000 per year says that imports of foreign steel should be reduced to save his job, what he really means is this: he wants to be protected from competition so that he can continue his present employment at the same or a higher salary, rather than move to a different job that has less desirable working conditions or pays a lower salary. There is nothing wrong with the steelworker's goal (better working conditions and higher pay), but it has nothing to do with "saving" jobs. (Despite this, we may use the term in the discussion that follows because it is such convenient shorthand.)

## The Gains from International Trade

In any discussion of the consequences of international trade restrictions, it is essential to remember two facts. First, *we pay for imports with exports.* It is true that, in the short run, we can sell off assets or borrow from abroad if we happen to import more goods and services than we export. But we have only a finite amount of assets to sell, and foreigners will not wait forever for us to pay our bills. Ultimately, our accounts can be settled only if we *provide* (export) goods and services to the trading partners from whom we *purchase* (import) goods and services. Trade, after all, involves a *quid pro quo* (literally, "something for something").

The second point to remember is that *voluntary trade is mutually beneficial to the trading partners.* If we restrict international trade, we reduce those benefits, both for our trading partners and for ourselves. One way these reduced benefits are manifested is in the form of curtailed employment opportunities for workers. The reasoning is simple. Other countries will buy our goods only if they can market theirs because they, too, have to export goods to pay for their imports. Thus, any U.S. restrictions on imports to this country—via tariffs, quotas, or other means—ultimately cause a reduction in our exports because other countries will be unable to pay for our goods. This implies that import restrictions inevitably must decrease the size of our export sector. So, imposing trade restrictions to save jobs in import-competing industries has the effect of costing jobs in export industries. Most studies have shown that the net effect seems to be reduced employment overall.

## The Adverse Effects of Trade Restrictions

Just as important, import restrictions impose costs on U.S. consumers as a whole. By reducing competition from abroad, quotas, tariffs, and other trade restraints push up the prices of foreign goods and enable U.S. producers to hike their own prices. Perhaps the best-documented example of this effect is found in the automobile industry, where "voluntary" restrictions on Japanese imports were in place for more than a decade.

Due in part to the enhanced quality of imported cars, sales of domestically produced automobiles fell from nine million units in 1978 to an average of six million units per year between 1980 and 1982. Profits of U.S. automakers plummeted as well, and some incurred substantial losses. The automobile manufacturers' and autoworkers' unions demanded protection from import competition. Politicians from automobile-producing states joined in their cries. The result was a "voluntary" agreement by Japanese car companies (the most important competitors of U.S. firms) to restrict their U.S. sales to 1.68 million units per year. This agreement—which amounted to a quota, even though it never officially bore that name—began in April 1981 and continued into the 1990s in various forms.

Robert W. Crandall, an economist with the Brookings Institution, estimated how much this voluntary trade restriction cost U.S. consumers, measured in terms of higher car prices. According to his estimates, the reduced supply of Japanese cars pushed their prices up by $1,500 per car, measured in 1996 dollars. The higher prices of Japanese imports, in turn, enabled domestic producers to hike their prices an average of $600 per car. The total tab in the first full year of the program was $6.5 billion. Crandall also estimated that about 26,000 jobs in automobile-related industries were saved by the voluntary import restrictions. Dividing $6.5 billion by 26,000 jobs yields a cost to consumers of more than $250,000 *per year* for every job saved in the automobile industry. U.S. consumers could have saved nearly $2 billion on their car purchases each year if, instead of implicitly agreeing to import restrictions, they had simply given $75,000 to every autoworker whose job was preserved by the voluntary import restraints.

The same types of calculations have been made for other industries. Tariffs in the apparel industry were increased between 1977 and 1981, saving the jobs of about 116,000 U.S. apparel workers at a cost of $45,000 per job each year. The cost of protectionism has been even higher in other industries. Jobs preserved in the glassware industry due to trade restrictions cost $200,000 apiece each year. In the maritime industry, the yearly cost of trade restriction is $270,000 per job. In the steel industry, the cost of preserving a job has been estimated at an astounding $750,000 *per year*. If free trade were permitted, each worker losing a job could be given a cash payment of half that amount each year, and consumers would still save a lot of wealth.

## The Real Impact on Jobs

Even so, this is not the full story. None of these cost studies has attempted to estimate the ultimate impact of import restrictions on the flow of exports, the number of jobs lost in the export sector, and thus the total number of jobs gained or lost.

Remember that imports pay for exports and that our imports are the exports of our trading partners. So, when imports to the United States are restricted, our trading partners will necessarily buy less of what we produce. The resulting decline in export sales means fewer jobs in exporting industries. And the total reduction in trade leads to fewer jobs for workers such as stevedores (who unload ships) and truck drivers (who carry goods to and from ports). On both counts— the overall cut in trade and the accompanying decline in exports—protectionism leads to job losses that might not be obvious immediately.

In 1983, Congress tried to pass a "domestic-content" bill for automobiles. In effect, the legislation would have required that cars sold in the United States have a minimum percentage of their components manufactured and assembled in this country. Proponents of the legislation argued that it would have protected 300,000 jobs in the U.S. automobile manufacturing and auto parts supply industries. Yet the legislation's supporters failed to recognize the negative impact of the bill on trade in general and its ultimate impact on U.S. export industries. A U.S. Department of Labor study did recognize these impacts, estimating that the domestic-content legislation would have cost more jobs in trade-related and export industries than it protected in import-competing businesses. Congress ultimately decided not to impose a domestic-content requirement for cars sold in the United States.

## The Long-Run Failure of Import Controls

In principle, trade restrictions are imposed to provide economic help to specific industries and to increase employment in those industries. Ironically, the long-term effects may be just the opposite. Researchers at the World Trade Organization (WTO) examined employment in three industries that have been heavily protected throughout the world—textiles, clothing, and iron and steel. Despite stringent protectionist measures, employment in these industries actually declined during the period of protection, in some cases dramatically. In textiles, employment fell 22 percent in the United States and 46 percent in the European Common Market (the predecessor of the European Union). Employment losses in the clothing industry ranged from 18 percent in the United States to 56 percent in Sweden. Losses in the iron and steel industry ranged from 10 percent in Canada to 54 percent in the United States. In short, the WTO researchers found that restrictions on free trade were no guarantee against job losses—even in the industries supposedly being protected.

The evidence seems clear: the cost of protecting jobs in the short run is enormous. And, in the long run, it appears that jobs cannot be protected, especially if one considers all aspects of protectionism. Free trade is a tough platform on which to run for office, but it is likely to be the one that will yield the most general benefits if implemented. Of course, this does not mean that politicians will embrace it. So we end up "saving" jobs at an annual cost of $750,000 each.

## For Critical Analysis

1. If it would be cheaper to give each steelworker $375,000 per year in cash than impose restrictions on steel imports, why do we have the import restrictions rather than the cash payments?
2. Most U.S. imports and exports travel through our seaports at some point. How do you predict that members of Congress from coastal states would vote on proposals to restrict international trade? What other information would you want to know in making such a prediction?
3. Who gains and who loses from import restrictions? In answering, you should consider both consumers and producers, in both the country that imposes the restrictions and in the other countries affected by them. Also, be sure to take into account the effects of import restrictions on *export* industries.

# 25

# *The Trade Revolution in Textiles*

A revolution is sweeping through the world textile industry. After decades of **protectionism,** on January 1, 2005 the complex web of textile **quotas** that protected manufacturers in the European Union (EU) and North America from overseas competition was essentially stripped away. The result is massive upheaval and relocation in an industry that employs more than forty million people around the world. For the United States and the EU, the results will be sharply lower textile production and textile prices. For China, India, and a few other nations, there is now a boom in textile manufacturing and employment. And for nations such as Bangladesh, Mauritius, and Vietnam, the future is clouded with uncertainty and with the prospect of lower incomes for people whose incomes are already among the lowest in the world.

## The Multifiber Agreement

Historically, clothing and textiles are among the first manufacturing activities in which developing nations invest, and

168

they are also among the first from which they depart as development proceeds. Textiles helped launch Great Britain into the Industrial Revolution, and textiles formed the backbone of the earliest American manufacturing enterprises of the nineteenth century. In the twentieth century, the developing nations of Central America, Asia, and elsewhere looked to textiles to start themselves on the path to modern economic development—much to the distress of textile firms and workers in Europe and North America.

Perhaps, partly because the industry has so often played a key role in economic development, it is one that has been plagued by protectionism. Whether imposed by developing nations to promote their infant textile industries, or by western nations trying to quash competition from elsewhere in the world, textile tariffs and quotas have been commonplace for the last two centuries.

In 1974, the signatories to the **Multifiber Agreement (MFA)** attempted to rationalize the crazy quilt of trade barriers in this industry, replacing them with a comprehensive system of quotas. These quotas specified, in extraordinary detail, which nation could send what textile products to each country that was a party to the MFA. Like all quotas, those of the MFA reduced the foreign supply of textiles to each importing nation. This, in turn, reduced the total market supply of textiles in each of those nations (most notably in Europe and North America, which form the major markets for textiles). As a result, the price of textiles rose in importing nations, which, in turn, had two further effects: domestic production of textiles within importing nations was stimulated by the higher prices, and this, in turn, meant both higher profits for firms, and higher wages and textile employment levels within importing nations. But the higher prices also reduced the welfare of consumers in Europe and North America, and discouraged consumption of clothing and other textiles in those nations. Indeed, the cost to consumers in America alone has been estimated at $70 billion per year, with the worst of the burden falling on low-income families, which tend to spend a larger share of their income on clothes.

On the other side of the world, the MFA cut deeply into the development prospects of dozens of nations. Low wages in developing countries helped give them a comparative advantage in textiles, but one that they could not fully exploit because of the MFA restrictions on where they could sell their goods. As a practical matter, by closing off markets to manufacturers in developing nations, the MFA depressed the prices firms could get for their products, and cut deeply into the wages and employment of workers there. It is estimated that the MFA cost developing nations some $40 billion per year in lost export revenues, and reduced employment in those countries by twenty-seven million—or thirty-five jobs lost for every textile job saved in the EU, Canada, and the United States.

On balance, the losses caused by the MFA vastly exceeded the gains enjoyed by groups, such as domestic producers, in importing nations. And these net losses occurred in both importing and exporting nations, for fundamentally the same reason: goods were no longer being supplied by the lowest cost producers, implying that resources were being wasted.

## Uruguay and the End of the MFA

In 1994, as part of the world trade agreements signed in Uruguay, agreement was reached to end the textile quotas, as of the end of 2004. Although these agreements left the EU, the United States, and other importing nations with some residual capacity to blunt and slow the effects of quota elimination, the worldwide transformation of the industry has already begun.

The long-term downward trend in textile manufacturing and employment in importing nations has accelerated sharply, as prices for textiles have fallen. In China, and to a lesser extent in India and a few other exporting nations, production is up sharply, as is textile employment and exports. The end of the MFA spells economic prosperity for them. But there are other exporting nations around the world, such as Bangladesh, Mauritius, and Vietnam, which—seemingly paradoxically—are suffering as a result of the elimination of textile quotas, because along with quotas, "quota-hopping" is disappearing as well.

## The Economics of Quota-Hopping

Under the MFA, each exporting nation received a quota allotment that specified the amount of clothing and other textiles that it could sell to each MFA-signatory nation. When China, for example, hit its quota of sales to the United States, then U.S. importers had to look elsewhere for textiles: they had to find a nation where suppliers had not yet exhausted their quota allotment. Thus, instead of being able to engage in "one-stop shopping," importers had to acquire goods from suppliers scattered around the globe, sometimes even having to split production processes for the same garments across different countries. This practice, of moving orders around the world to nations with available quota allotment, came to be called **quota-hopping.**

For employers and workers in many developing nations, quota-hopping was an essential ingredient of their livelihood. Suppliers in many smaller countries lived off the overflow business created when manufacturers in China and India bumped up against their countries' quota limits. Indeed, the textile industry of the island nation of Mauritius arguably owed its entire existence to quota-hopping. And although Bangladesh long has been a textile exporter, it is generally acknowledged that much of that nation's textile industry has been supported by its guaranteed access to European and U.S. markets under the MFA quota system.

For importers of textiles, the necessity to engage in quota-hopping drove up costs and turned their distribution chains into logistical nightmares. Costs were elevated partly because the quotas prevented the most efficient manufacturers of textiles from supplying world demands. But there was an additional reason: the elaborate system of quotas meant that buyers often had to purchase fabric in one nation, have it cut in another country, and then have the pieces assembled into clothing in, yet, a third nation. Thousands of miles of additional travel and numerous added steps of  handling and record-keeping made supply chains extraordinarily complex and costly. Consumers paid higher prices for their clothes and producers received lower profits for their efforts.

## Revolution

The end of quotas obviously means the end of quota-hopping—and the end of textile jobs in many places. In Bangladesh, where textile exports have accounted for more than 75 percent of that nation's *total* exports, it is expected that without the protection afforded by quota-hopping, textile exports will drop by 25 to 40 percent within just a few years. And the entire textile industry of Mauritius is rapidly disappearing in its entirety. In the United States, a major textile importer, it is likely that the end of quotas will cause textile employment to drop 60 to 70 percent between 2004 and 2010.

Of course there are some winners in the game. China, for example, is poised to increase its market share to 50 percent by 2008 from its 2004 level of 25 percent. India also is expecting a surge in business, although for a variety of reasons the future is less clear there. For example, restrictive labor practices in India make it almost impossible for firms with more than one hundred employees to fire workers, thereby driving up costs. Similarly, India's notoriously poor infrastructure (ranging from dirt roads to antiquated port facilities) not only raises costs, but also slows the response of Indian manufacturers to changes in market conditions.

Indeed, speed and flexibility are crucial in an industry where fashions rarely outlast the year. Manufacturers in Turkey and Mexico are counting on their proximity to the EU and the United States, respectively, to help them weather the revolution. These neighboring suppliers can deliver goods made to fresh designs in a matter of six weeks, rather than the six months that is commonplace for China. As a result, many of the textile firms in these nations are likely to survive, despite having costs that are significantly higher than those of their Chinese and Indian competitors.

As this example illustrates, not everything in textiles is driven purely by costs. For example, although clothing and textile employment in Italy has been cut by the elimination of quotas, the remaining firms have focused profitably on niche markets where style, luxury, and high quality are paramount. In the United States, it is high tech that has proven to be the safe haven, with firms using the latest in computers and chemicals to carve out markets in products ranging from disposable surgical gowns to decontamination suits impermeable to deadly viruses.

It is not just selected supplying nations that are winners: consumers likely will gain the most. China's expansion into textiles during the late 1990s and early 2000s helped drive U.S. clothing prices down more than 30 percent in inflation-adjusted terms. China's further expansion in the aftermath of quotas is putting even more downward pressure on prices, broadening the range of goods available to consumers, and shortening the time lag from drawing board to dressing room.

## Falling Off a Cliff

The biggest drive to simplify distribution systems has come from major chains, such as Wal-Mart, which have responded to the end of quotas by concentrating their purchases in only a few nations, with China being the most-favored nation. Because the United States accounts for one-third of the world's textile imports, and major chains such as Wal-Mart supply much of the U.S. market, the result has been massive consolidation of supply sources.

In addition, both the United States and the EU (the other major textile importer) did their best between 1994 and 2004 to delay the implementation of the new trade rules for textiles. Although this elevated domestic textile employment and profits in both locales, it also made the move to a quota-free system that much more difficult. Thus, even though firms, workers, and politicians had a decade to anticipate the end of quotas, the impact of the change is still "like falling off a cliff" according to one observer.

Still, there is no doubt about two things. First, the world's textile consumers are clearly better off without textile quotas. Prices are lower, selection is greater, and innovation has enhanced style and quality. Second, the end of the MFA has raised the wealth of the world as a whole. Lower costs, greater consumption, and improved quality all have contributed to an elevated standard of living. Indeed, if economists at the World Bank and International Monetary Fund are to be believed, world income will be nearly $140 billion higher per year because we are no longer saddled with textile quotas. Even with all its accompanying upheaval, the revolution in textiles illustrates, once again, that voluntary trade creates wealth.

## For Critical Analysis

1. If quotas harm the consumers in a nation that imposes them, why does that nation's government take such an action?
2. Imports of sugar into the United States, like imports of textiles, long have been subject to quotas. The United States is a major market for both textiles and sugar. What impact have quotas on these goods likely had on prices of these goods elsewhere in the world? What impact, on average, has this had on countries that export these goods? How do you think this might have changed the way they view the United States?
3. A quota limits the amount supplied by a group of suppliers to a fixed amount, regardless of price. Using demand and supply analysis, show how this affects the following: (i) the total supply of the good to a nation, including both domestic supply and the foreign supply that is limited by the quota; (ii) the market price of the good in the nation imposing the quota; (iii) consumption of the affected good in that nation; and (iv) the well-being of that nation's consumers and domestic suppliers.

# The Trade Deficit

The idea is not new. Indeed, it goes back centuries. Selling to foreigners is better than buying from them. That is, exports are good and imports are bad. Today, reading between the lines of the press coverage about international trade reveals that political and public thinking is not much different than it was three hundred years ago. The **mercantilists** who ruled public policy from the sixteenth through eighteenth centuries felt that the only proper objective of international trade was to expand exports without expanding imports. Their goal was to acquire large amounts of the gold that served as the money of their era. The mercantilists felt that a **trade surplus** (an excess of goods and service exports over imports) was the only way a nation could gain from trade. This same idea is expressed by modern day patriots who reason that "If I buy a Sony laptop computer from Japan, I have the laptop and Japan has the money. On the other hand, if I buy a Dell laptop in the United States, I have the laptop and the United States has the money. Thus, I should 'Buy American'." This sort of reasoning leads to the conclusion that the persistent international trade deficit that the United States experiences year after year is bad for America. Let's see if this conclusion makes any sense.

## Modern Day Mercantilists

During any given month, you cannot fail to see headlines about our continuing (or growing) **trade deficit.** Even if you are not quite sure how to actually calculate our international trade deficit, you might guess that the problem seems to be that we are importing more than we are exporting.

To understand the actual numbers reported in the press, you must understand that there are several components of trade deficits. The most obvious part of a trade deficit consists of merchandise exports and imports. This is the number that receives the most coverage in the press. Look at the following table. There you see the merchandise (or goods) trade deficit for the United States for a recent ten-year period.

### Exports and Imports of Goods (billions of dollars)

| Year | Exports | Imports | Deficit |
| --- | --- | --- | --- |
| 1994 | 502.9 | −668.7 | −165.8 |
| 1995 | 575.2 | −749.4 | −174.2 |
| 1996 | 612.1 | −803.1 | −191.0 |
| 1997 | 678.4 | −876.5 | −198.1 |
| 1998 | 670.4 | −917.1 | −246.7 |
| 1999 | 684.0 | −1,030.0 | −346.0 |
| 2000 | 772.0 | −1,224.4 | −452.4 |
| 2001 | 718.7 | −1,145.9 | −427.2 |
| 2002 | 681.9 | −1,164.7 | −482.9 |
| 2003 | 713.1 | −1,260.7 | −547.6 |
| 2004 | 775.6 | −1,378.8 | −603.1 |

Source: Council of Economic Advisers, *Economic Report of the President* (sums may not add to totals due to rounding; figures for 2004 are preliminary estimates)

It looks pretty bad, doesn't it? It seems as if we've become addicted to imports! But merchandise is not the only thing that we buy and sell abroad. Increasingly, service exports and imports account for a major aspect of international trade, at least in the United States. (Some of the types of services we export involve accounting, legal research, investment advice, travel and transportation, and medical research.) For these and other service items, even mercantilists would be happy to know that the United States consistently exports more than it imports, as you can see in the following table, which shows the *net* balance of trade for the various categories of services.

## Net Exports of Services (billions of dollars)

| Year | Net Service Exports |
|------|---------------------|
| 1994 | 68.7 |
| 1995 | 79.1 |
| 1996 | 88.1 |
| 1997 | 91.2 |
| 1998 | 83.5 |
| 1999 | 84.8 |
| 2000 | 77.0 |
| 2001 | 69.4 |
| 2002 | 64.8 |
| 2003 | 51.1 |
| 2004 | 57.2 |

Source: Council of Economic Advisers, *Economic Report of the President* (figures for 2004 are preliminary estimates)

## The Link Between Imports and Exports

Obviously, a comparison of the two tables still shows a substantial trade deficit, no matter how many times you look at the numbers. Should residents of the United States be worried? Before we can answer this question, we must look at some basic propositions about the relationship between imports and exports.

We begin by considering how we pay for the foreign goods and services that we import. Countries do not ship goods to the United States simply to hold pieces of paper in exchange.

Businesses in the rest of the world ship us goods and services because they want goods and services in exchange. That means only one thing, then: *In the long run, we pay for imports with exports. Thus, in the long run, imports must equal exports.* The short run is a different story, of course. Imports can be paid for by the sale of real and financial assets, such as land, stocks, and bonds, or through an extension of credit from other countries. But in the long run, foreigners eventually want goods and services in return for goods and services they send us. Consumption is, after all, the ultimate objective of production.

Because imports are paid for with exports, in the long run any attempt to reduce this country's trade deficit by restricting imports must also impact exports. In fact, a direct corollary of our first proposition must be that *any restrictions on imports must ultimately lead to a reduction in exports.* Thus, every time politicians call for a reduction in our trade deficit, they are implicitly calling for a reduction in exports, at least in the long run.

It is possible that politicians don't understand this, but even if they did, they might still call for restricting imports. After all, it is easy for the domestic firms that lose business to foreign competition to claim that every dollar of imports represents a lost dollar of sales for them—implying, of course, a corresponding reduction in U.S. employment. In contrast, the tens of thousands of exporters of U.S. goods and services probably won't ever be able to put an exact value on their reduced sales and employment due to proposed and actual import restrictions. Hence, the people with "evidence" about the supposed harms of imports will always outnumber those businesses who lose export sales when international trade is restricted.

## A Renegade View of Imports?

Many discussions about international trade have to do with the supposed "unfairness" of imports. Somehow (it is argued), when goods come in from a foreign land, the result is unfair to the firms and workers who must compete with those imports. To see how such reasoning is not reasoning at all, one must only consider a simple example.

Assume you have just discovered a way to produce textiles at one-tenth the cost of your closest competitors, who are located in South Carolina. You set up your base of operations in Florida and start selling your textiles at lower prices than your South Carolina competitors do. Your workers are appreciative of their jobs and your shareholders are appreciative of their profits. To be sure, the textile owners and employees in South Carolina may not be happy, but there is nothing legally they can do about it. This, of course, is the essence of unfettered trade among the fifty states: production takes place where costs are lowest and consumers benefit from the lower prices that result.

Now let's assume that you build the same facility in Florida, but instead of actually producing the textiles yourself, you secretly have them brought from South Africa to sell, as before, at lower prices than those at which the South Carolina firms can profitably produce. If everyone continues to believe that you are producing the textiles on your own, there will be no problems. But if anybody finds out that you are importing the textiles, then the political wrath of members of Congress from South Carolina will descend on you. They will try to prohibit the importation of "cheap" textiles from South Africa, or put a high tax, called a **tariff,** on those textiles.

Is there really any difference between these two "production processes"? The first one involves the use of some textile machinery within the United States; whereas the second "production process" involves having a ship and some trucks pick up the textiles and drop them off at the "factory" in Florida. But are they really any different? We think not. Such is the conclusion when using positive economic analysis. Once the world of politics gets involved, however, the domestic production process is favored and the production process that involves imports is frowned upon.

## The Other Side of Trade Deficits

Most discussions of the trade deficit are further flawed by the fact that they completely ignore the mirror image of the deficit. In the short run, when exports of goods and services don't match up dollar-for-dollar for imports, the trading partners involved clearly must be making arrangements for short-run methods to pay for the difference. Thus, for example, when the United States is importing more goods and services than it is exporting, we must be selling real and financial assets to our trading partners. For example, we might be borrowing from abroad (selling bonds), or selling shares of stock in U.S. corporations. (In the late 1990s, we also sold real estate, such as golf courses and office buildings.)

Now, at first blush, this sounds like we are "mortgaging the future," selling assets and borrowing funds in order to consume more now. But there is a different way to look at this: America is the safest, most productive place in the world to invest. *If the rest of the world is to be able to invest in the United States, we must run a trade deficit.* This proposition is a simple matter of arithmetic.

When, say, a South Korean automobile company builds a factory in the United States, there is an inflow of funds from South Korea to the United States. When foreign residents buy U.S. government securities, there is an inflow of funds from other countries to the United States. These investments are usually called private capital flows, and they include private land purchases, acquisitions of corporate stock shares, and purchases of government bonds. Virtually every year for the past thirty years, foreign residents have invested more in the United States than U.S. residents have invested abroad. This net inflow of capital funds from abroad is called a **capital account surplus.**

As a glance at Figure 26-1 reveals, this net inflow of investment funds into the United States essentially mirrors the trade deficit that the United States experiences each year. That is, when the current account trade deficit is small, the capital account surplus is small, and when the current account deficit is large, so, too, is the capital account surplus. Is this just a coincidence? Certainly not. Think about it. If a foreign resident wants to buy stock in a U.S. company, that foreign resident must obtain dollars to pay for the stock. While it is true that the foreign resident simply goes to the foreign exchange market to do so, these dollars must somehow get supplied to the foreign exchange market. That supply of dollars must, in turn, come from the excess of imports over

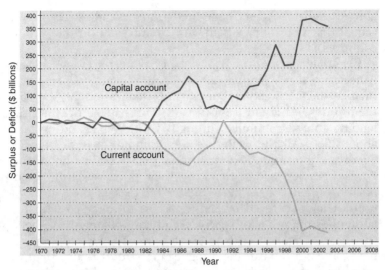

**Figure 26-1. The Relationship Between the Current Account and the Capital Account**

exports each year. In other words: *our international trade deficit supplies the dollars in foreign exchange markets necessary for foreigners to invest in the United States.* If Americans did not import more goods and services than they export, foreign residents could not invest in the United States.

## The Sweep of History

Contrary to what you might think from reading the papers, although the United States has been running a trade deficit for the last twenty-five years, this is not the first time we have run such a deficit over a long period of time. Indeed, from the Civil War until World War I, the United States ran a trade deficit year after year, borrowing funds and selling corporate stock all around the world. Were the consequences disastrous? Hardly. We used the funds we obtained from abroad to build railroads and steel mills and much of the rest of our industrial base, as well as to settle the West. We benefitted from having access to low-cost finance (which we used to purchase key goods from abroad) and foreigners benefitted from risk-adjusted rates of return that were higher than they could obtain in their home countries.

Beginning in World War I this pattern reversed itself. Americans began lending money to Europeans to help them finance their war expenditures, and, then, after the war lent them funds to rebuild from the war. This pattern of American lending abroad continued through World War II and on until about 1980. All the while, we were running a trade surplus, exporting more goods and services than we were importing. Foreign residents were financing their purchases from us by borrowing and by selling us shares of stock in their corporations. They benefitted by getting access to lower cost finance and goods than they otherwise could have obtained. We benefitted by selling our goods at a better price than we could get at home and also by earning a higher net rate of return than we could have obtained if we had invested only in domestic assets.

Thus, we see that the trade deficits of the last quarter century are, importantly, a return to the pattern of the late nineteenth century and early twentieth century. Again, the United States is the nation offering the highest risk-adjusted return—so foreigners invest here. There is one key difference between now and one hundred years ago, however. Back then, virtually all of the borrowing was being done by the private sector, so one could be reasonably certain that it was going to turn out to yield net benefits. Today, much of the borrowing is being done by the U.S. government. Will this turn out to yield net benefits? Only time will tell.


## For Critical Analysis

1. Why can't competing producers in different states prevent "imports" into their own state? (HINT: What document was written over two hundred years ago?)
2. How does the concept of "Buy Local" relate to concerns about trade deficits on an international basis?
3. Does it matter to you where the product you are buying has been manufactured? Why or why not?

# 27

# *The Dollar Standard*

Twenty years ago, when the Japanese economy was booming, many economists declared that Japan's currency, the yen, would become a world reserve currency, just like the dollar. Ten years ago, when plans for the adoption of the common currency in Europe—the euro—were put into high gear, many of the same commentators declared that this new currency would at least equal the importance of the U.S. dollar in the world financial markets. In the early 2000s, as the U.S. economy struggled through a recession, the dollar's role as the leading financial unit of accounting was again questioned. After all, the United States was continuing to import much more than it was exporting, the federal government budget was suffering serious deficits, and fears of more terrorist attacks were everywhere.

A funny thing happened on the way to the bank. The dollar, though not as strong as it was in the late 1990s, has remained the *de facto* monetary standard throughout the world. In other words, the U.S. dollar remains the currency of choice in many international transactions, though no central bank or international body, such as the World Bank, has ever officially acknowledged its position.

## The Meaning of the *De Facto* Dollar Standard

What does it mean to call the dollar the *de facto* standard for the world's financial system? First, consider what it means domestically, within our own borders, for the dollar to be our **monetary standard.** It means that the dollar is the **medium of exchange,** as well as a **store of value** and a **unit of accounting.** To be sure, the U.S. dollar does not perform these same functions in most other countries. They use their own domestic currency—pesos, rubles, yen, pounds—as a medium of exchange and often as a store of value and a unit of accounting.

Nonetheless, in international transactions, the dollar remains the medium of exchange for trade in a wide variety of commodities, including oil and many primary metals. The dollar also remains the medium of exchange for many industrial goods and for many services. What does that role mean exactly? Suppose that a gasoline refinery in China wants to buy crude oil on the world market. When the purchasing agent of the refinery looks up the price on the Internet, she sees that it is stated in U.S. dollars per barrel of crude oil. Normally, that purchasing agent will have to come up with dollars to purchase the crude oil, too. Even within the euro zone (sometimes called Euroland), only 40 percent of commercial transactions are billed in euros; the rest are billed in good old U.S. dollars.

In foreign exchange markets, the dollar also remains the benchmark against which different foreign currencies are measured, or priced. When a bank or other entity wishes to purchase or sell a foreign currency for delivery in the future—called a **forward foreign exchange transaction**—the currency to be purchased or sold is usually priced in terms of its U.S. dollar cost. For example, if you wished to buy Indian rupees or Thai baht for delivery ninety days from now, you would find that their forward prices are listed in terms of dollars, not some other currency, such as euros or yen.

The dollar, it seems, is everywhere. When financial capital flows across borders, no matter where those borders are, most of this capital is denominated in U.S. dollars. When non-European governments want to support the value of their own currencies, they do so by selling some of their dollar reserves in order to buy back their own currency in foreign exchange markets. When it comes to being an international store of value, nothing can touch the greenback.

## The Dollar Is a Reserve Currency

In the United States, banks typically hold reserves in the form of dollars on deposit at Federal Reserve banks or dollars (cash) held in their own vaults. Domestically, the U.S. dollar is obviously our **reserve currency.** But it also serves this function for many foreign central banks as well as for many foreign governments. They may not necessarily hold actual dollar bills, but they will hold the next best asset—U.S. Treasury bonds, which are denominated in dollars. By one estimate, 50 percent of all U.S. Treasury bonds are held as reserves in central banks throughout the world.

Historically, the British pound was a reserve currency during the nineteenth and early twentieth centuries. Since World War II, the mighty greenback has been the *de facto* reserve currency of choice throughout the world. It still appears to hold that position despite the numerous problems experienced by the U.S. economy in the early 2000s.

According to the International Monetary Fund (IMF), the yen, touted only twenty years ago as the next supercurrency, comprises only 5 percent of central bank reserves around the world. The euro does somewhat better at 19 percent of all central bank reserves. But here as elsewhere, the dollar is king, comprising 67 percent of central bank reserves around the world.

## Why Has the World Remained on a Dollar Standard?

Consider that one important stock market average, the Nasdaq, reached its peak in 2000. Over the next two years, it plummeted in value by more than two-thirds. Over the same period, another major U.S. stock market average, the Standard & Poors 500, declined in value by 40 percent. Economic growth in the United States, measured by either industrial production or real

GDP, stagnated. Nonetheless, the dollar remained the *de facto* international monetary standard in world financial markets and for world primary commodity dealings. Why?

The simple answer is that even though the U.S. economy may have done poorly in the early 2000s, the rest of the world did even worse. The great surge forward in the European Union (EU) that was predicted after the introduction of the euro on January 1, 2002, never happened. Indeed, the EU remains saddled with 9 percent unemployment rates and very low economic growth rates. Japan has fared no better. In Latin America, one country after another has defaulted on its international debt obligations.

By one estimate, even though the U.S. economy accounts for only a bit over 20 percent of total world output, it has contributed almost 40 percent of total world growth since the mid-1990s. Just as important, although the United States has not had the lowest inflation rate of any country in the world, its inflation rate has been well below the world average.

Everything is relative, including financial security across countries. While no one expects the U.S. economy to roar back to its superheated condition of the late 1990s, the world consensus seems to be that the United States will solve its economic problems more quickly than other countries. Moreover, the U.S. record for political stability is enviable by any standards. The essence of democracy is the peaceful transition from one government to another, and the United States seems to have mastered that process as well as anyone, enabling any and all that would invest in the United States or hold U.S. currency to do so with confidence.

The bottom line, then, is that the mighty greenback has three very powerful forces on its side. First, the U.S. economy is a huge part of the world economy, which means that in the course of conducting ordinary business in the international marketplace, many people have to use dollars—and to use them, one must hold them. Second, even though the U.S. economy and political system are not without their weaknesses, they rank among the best in the world by anyone's standards. Finally, the U.S. inflation rate has been both low and stable, meaning that people can have confidence in the dollar's future purchasing power. On all three counts, then, there is continued confidence in U.S. greenbacks and U.S. government securities, such as Treasury bonds. Let proponents of the yen, the euro, or even the pound say what they will: the dollar remains the closest thing we have to a world monetary standard.

## For Critical Analysis

1. The European financial community, including central bankers throughout Europe, made a big push in the early 2000s for the euro to be at least on a par with the U.S. dollar in international transactions. Why didn't these individuals succeed in their effort to get the rest of the world to, say, start quoting oil prices in euros?

2. Does it matter to you, as a resident of the United States, whether the U.S. dollar is the *de facto* international monetary standard?

3. During 2003 and 2004, two notable events affected world currency markets. First, the value of the dollar fell about 20 percent relative to most other major currencies, including the euro. Second, disputes arose among several of the nations who use the euro as their monetary unit, regarding appropriate monetary and fiscal policy with the European Union. Explain how each of these developments might affect the willingness of people around the world to use the U.S. dollar (rather than, say, the euro) as a *de facto* monetary standard.

# 28

# *The Euro: Promise and Peril*

For twelve major European nations, New Year's Day 2002 was truly "out with the old, in with the new." That was the day the euro became the common currency for most members of the **European Union (EU),** replacing some $600 billion worth of francs, marks, lira, and other national currencies with a common currency controlled by the newly created European Central Bank. For Americans traveling to Europe, the switch to the euro has made life better, eliminating the need to keep track of a host of exchange rates and making it much easier to compare the prices of goods in different countries. Citizens of the twelve nations that have adopted the euro are enjoying those same benefits, but they are subject to more of the risks associated with the new currency—risks that some fear could overwhelm the lower transaction costs and greater convenience of having a single money for three hundred million people.

## The Benefits of a Single Currency

The notion of a single monetary system for Europe dates back at least as far as 1940, when Adolf Hitler proposed a "Bank of

Europe." Not until 1969, however, did European nations actually decide to seriously investigate the feasibility of a common currency. In 1991, the Maastricht Treaty was signed, marking a formal agreement to have a common currency. Many nations wanted to name the new (but as yet hypothetical) currency the ECU, which stood for European Currency Unit. The Germans objected, however; one of their complaints was that this would sound too much like "Eku," a German beer. Not until 1995 was the name *euro* approved. Finally, on January 1, 2002, ten billion bank notes and thousands of tons of coins made their way into circulation across Europe, beginning a two-month process in which the euro gradually displaced the national currencies of the twelve nations adopting it.

The push to create the euro was largely driven by the substantial costs and inconvenience of having many different currencies in a place as economically integrated as Europe. Every time individuals or businesses wanted to transact with someone in another country, they had to make price comparisons involving multiple currencies, convert payments or receipts between a foreign currency and their own, and insure themselves against the risks of holding foreign currencies subject to fluctuations in value. You can get a sense of the problem by imagining what it would be like if every state across the United States had a different currency. Interstate travel and trade would be a costly nuisance, fraught with risk and inconvenience. Just as Americans benefit from having the dollar as our single currency, the nations adopting the euro benefit from that currency. Overall, experts think, the European adopters of the new monetary unit are saving perhaps 0.5 percent of national income each year—roughly $120 per year for each person.

## The Costs of a Single Currency

Yet there are risks and, thus, potential costs associated with the adoption of a single currency. Broadly speaking, flexibility and independence are the great advantages of having a separate currency with a value that is free to fluctuate against other currencies. Let's consider flexibility first, by contrasting the United

Kingdom, a nation that chose not to adopt the euro, with France, which opted to give up the franc in return for the euro. If the demand for British goods declines, this also implicitly represents a decline in the demand for British currency (the pound), because if foreigners are not buying British goods, there is no reason for them to acquire pounds. One simple way for the United Kingdom to adjust to the drop in demand is to allow the value of the pound to fall relative to other currencies. This will make British goods cheaper in other countries and thus help counteract the lower demand for British products.

Let's contrast this scenario with the situation in France, which is using the euro. Because France is only a small part of the sum of the economies using the euro, if the demand for French goods declines, the value of the euro will decline little if at all. Hence, the French are forced to respond to the shock in one of two other (and more costly) ways. France must either endure a **deflation**—a fall in the prices of goods and services throughout France relative to elsewhere—or wait until factors of production, such as labor, leave the country to find employment elsewhere. Both of these processes are likely to be more painful and protracted than the simple expedient of allowing the exchange rate to decline, as the British are able to do. Our conclusion, then, is that a country with a separate currency has much more flexibility in responding to external shocks, for it can allow its exchange rate to vary, rather than having to wait for domestic prices or factors of production to move. This loss of flexibility is one of the costs of adopting the euro.

There is also the matter of independence. Consider, for example, the contrast between Germany and Greece. For whatever reason, for the past half century, the Bundesbank—the **central bank** of Germany—has chosen a relatively slow rate of monetary growth, which has led to a very low **inflation** rate in Germany. In contrast, the central bank of Greece has opted for a relatively high rate of growth in that nation's **money supply,** and thus a relatively high inflation rate in Greece—five times higher than Germany's rate during the 1990s alone. Under the European Central Bank, both Germany and Greece (as well as the other member nations) are stuck with a common monetary policy. We cannot know now what that policy will be, but given the historical differences between the policies of the countries involved, some nations are already looking at a monetary policy that is very different from the policy to which they are accustomed—and one that is, thus, likely to be quite painful for their citizens. For better or worse, by not adopting the euro, the British have retained the independence to make their own monetary policy and thus have avoided one of the costs of having a common currency.

## Optimal Currency Areas

The trade-offs involved in adopting the euro are central to the issue of defining an **optimal currency area.** The larger the economic area covered by a common currency, the greater the potential benefits (due to the facilitation of international trade), but the greater the potential costs (due to the reduced flexibility and independence), too. The real question concerns where the marginal benefits equal the marginal costs. The United States, for example, basically has been a single currency area since its inception. Yet, according to Professor Hugh Rockoff of Rutgers, until about seventy years ago, the benefits of having a common currency were probably outweighed by the costs. Different areas of the country, such as the agrarian South and West versus the industrial North and East, were simply far too different from each other; moreover, there were no mechanisms in place to reconcile the differences in desired monetary policies. Some experts believe that the euro currency area is likewise too big, with a set of member nations that are simply too different to permit the euro to work. Indeed, the desire to avoid the political and economic frictions that are sure to arise is likely an important reason why Britain, Sweden, and Denmark opted to stay out—at least for the moment.

## Still Number Two

Apart from the desire to facilitate trade among member nations, European nations had another incentive to agree to a common currency. As things stand today, the U.S. dollar is the premier "trading currency" of the world. That is, many businesses and people around the world use the dollar when conducting international trade, even though they stick with their own national currencies at home. To do this, of course, these economic agents must hold balances of dollars—either cash or bank accounts—which effectively act as interest-free loans to the United States. Thus, the United States is able to enjoy a higher level of income simply because our currency is held in such high regard around the world. There is little doubt that the nations adopting the euro hope it will someday rival or surpass the dollar as an international trading currency, enabling them to reap some of the benefits the United States has enjoyed. So far, however, as we saw in Chapter 27, most people around the world have decided that the dollar is still their best bet for a trading currency. For all the hopes and aspirations of its creators, the euro is still only number two in the world monetary arena.

This brings us to the other reason that may have helped persuade Britain to eschew the euro. Until World War II, the British pound was a major trading currency around the world, especially in Britain's former colonies. If the euro fails because of internal divisions among the countries using it, the British pound will likely be the only European currency left standing to challenge the dollar as a trading currency. And quite apart from national pride, there is little doubt that the citizens of the United Kingdom would like nothing better than the added income that would mean—especially if it came at the expense of some of their rivals across the English Channel.

## For Critical Analysis

1. Many European nations have government restrictions that impede the mobility of labor across national borders. How do these restrictions affect the desirability of having a common currency area in those countries?

2. Until about thirty years ago, many nations chose to have **fixed exchange rates,** in which the value of their domestic currency was fixed at a specified number of U.S. dollars.

How did the United States benefit from this system? To what sort of risks were other countries subjected because they had fixed exchange rates with the dollar?

3. The European Union (EU) recently expanded to twenty-five members and may have grown even larger by the time you read this. The economies of the new members are much different than the economies of the original members of the EU. How will this fact affect (i) the chance that these new members will want to use the euro as their monetary unit and (ii) the amount of friction within the EU about appropriate monetary and fiscal policy?

# Glossary

**absenteeism:** the incidence of job absences by employees due to illness or other events

**aggregate demand:** the total value of all planned spending on goods and services by all economic entities in the economy

**amnesty:** a general pardon for past offenses, such as illegally residing in the United States

**appropriations bills:** legislation that determines the size of government discretionary spending

**asset:** any valuable good capable of yielding flows of income or services over time

**asset market:** any institution or market in which purchases and sales of claims to future income or services are traded; for example, the housing market and the stock market

**average duration of unemployment:** the average number of weeks that unemployed persons spend unemployed

**bank run:** an attempt by many of a bank's depositors to convert checkable and savings deposits into currency because of a perceived fear for the bank's solvency

**bankruptcy:** a state of being legally declared unable to pay one's debts, so that some or all of the indebtedness is legally wiped out by the courts

**bilateral:** pertaining to two-way agreements or exchanges, as in bilateral trade agreements, which are entered into and apply only to two nations

**bond:** a debt; the right to receive a specific series of money payments in the future

**bondholders:** the owners of government or corporate bonds

**bubble:** when used in reference to asset prices, an episode in which those prices exceed their values based on economic fundamentals, as determined by real future profits or service flows

**budget constraint:** all of the possible combinations of goods that can be purchased at given prices and given income

**budget deficit:** the excess of government spending over government revenues during a given time period

**business cycles:** the ups and downs in overall business activity, evidenced by changes in GDP, employment, and the price level

**business investment:** purchases by firms of newly produced capital goods or inventories

**capital account surplus:** net inflow of capital funds (loans and investments) into a nation

**capital gain:** a rise in the market (capital) value of an asset, such as a share of stock

**capital stock:** the collection of productive assets that can be combined with other inputs, such as labor, to produce goods and services

**central bank:** a banker's bank, usually a government institution that also serves as the country's treasury's bank. Central banks normally regulate commercial banks

**checkable deposits:** accounts at depository institutions that are payable on demand, either by means of a check or by direct withdrawal, such as through an automated teller machine (ATM)

**civil law system:** a legal system in which statutes passed by legislatures and executive decrees, rather than judicial decisions based on precedent, form the basis for most legal rules

**common law system:** a legal system in which judicial decisions based on precedent, rather than executive decrees or statutes passed by legislatures, form the basis for most legal rules

**comparative advantage:** the ability to produce a good or service at a lower opportunity cost compared to other producers

**compensating wage premium:** additional wages demanded by workers to get them to accept unpleasant or hazardous working conditions

**consumer price index (CPI):** a measure of the dollar cost of purchasing a bundle of goods and services supposed to be representative of the consumption pattern of a typical consumer; one measure of the price level

**consumption:** spending by consumers on new goods and services

**corporate dividends:** payments made by corporations to the individuals who own stock in those corporations

**corporate income taxes:** taxes paid by corporations on the income they earn on their operations

**cost:** the highest-valued forgone alternative; the best option sacrificed when a choice is made

**cost of living:** the dollar cost (relative to a base year) of achieving a given level of satisfaction

**creditor:** an institution or individual that is owed money by another institution or individual

**currency:** paper and coins issued by the government to serve as a medium of exchange

**deflation:** a decline in the average level of the prices of goods and services

**demand:** the willingness and ability to purchase goods

**depository institutions:** financial institutions that accept deposits from savers and lend those deposits out to borrowers

**direct foreign investment:** resources provided to individuals and firms in a nation by individuals or firms located in other countries, often taking the form of foreign subsidiary or branch operations of a parent company

**disability payments:** cash payments made to persons whose physical or mental disabilities prevent them from working

**discouraged workers:** persons who have dropped out of the labor force because they are unable to find suitable work

**discretionary spending:** government spending that is decided upon anew each year, rather than being driven by a formula or set of rules

**disposable income:** income remaining after all taxes, retirement contributions, and the like are deducted

**dividends:** payments made by a corporation to owners of shares of its stock, generally based on the corporation's profits

**drift:** the average annual rate at which stock prices change over a long period of time

**dumping:** the sale of goods in a foreign country at a price below the market price charged for the same goods in the domestic market, or at a price below the cost of production

**e-cash:** money balances recorded on smart cards and computer drives

**economic growth:** sustained increases in real per capita income

**economic resources:** all items that are either of direct consumption value to individuals or can be used to produce other items that can be consumed

**electronic payments systems:** the use of electronically transmitted digital information to settle transactions

**entitlement programs:** government programs for which spending is determined chiefly by formulas or rules that specify who is eligible for funds and how much they may receive

**entrepreneurs:** individuals who seek to develop innovative products and methods of organizing businesses and serving customers

**equity:** assets minus liabilities; net asset value

**escalator clauses:** contractual provisions specifying that nominal (or dollar) amounts are to be adjusted upward or downward in proportion to some agreed-upon measure of the price level

**European Union (EU):** an agreement among the major European nations to closely integrate the economic, political, and legal systems of their individual nations

**expansion:** a period in which economic activity, measured by industrial production, employment, real income, and wholesale-retail sales, is growing on a sustained basis

**expected rate of inflation:** the rate at which the average level of prices of goods and services is expected to rise

**external debt:** debt owed to persons outside a nation

**federal funds rate:** the nominal interest rate at which banks can borrow reserves from one another

**Federal Reserve System (the Fed):** the central bank of the United States

**fiscal policy:** discretionary changes in government spending or taxes so as to alter the overall state of the economy, including employment, investment, and output

**fiscal year:** the accounting year used by a government or business; for the federal government, the fiscal year runs from October 1 to September 30

**fixed costs:** costs that do not vary with the level of output

**fixed exchange rates:** a system of legally fixed prices (rates) at which two or more national currencies trade (exchange) for one another

**forward foreign exchange transaction:** a trade in which two parties agree to exchange two currencies at a date in the future at an exchange rate specified today

**gains from trade:** the extent to which individuals, firms, or nations benefit from engaging in voluntary exchange

**government-backed debt:** privately issued debt obligations that are either explicitly or implicitly guaranteed by a government

**gross domestic product (GDP):** the dollar value of all new, domestically produced final goods and services in an economy

**gross public debt:** includes all public debt, even that owned by agencies of the government issuing it

**historical cost:** the original purchase price of an asset

**human capital:** the productive capacity of human beings

**illiquid:** a financial condition in which one has insufficient cash on hand to meet one's current liabilities

**income:** claims to consumption

**inflation:** a rise in the average level of the prices of goods and services

**inflation targeting:** a policy in which the monetary authority sets a target or objective for the inflation rate and then adjusts policy instruments (such as growth in the money supply) to try to achieve that target

**inflation tax:** the decline in the real, or purchasing power, value of money balances due to inflation

**inflationary premium:** in percent per year, the additional premium that people are willing to pay to have dollars sooner rather than later simply because inflation is expected in the future

**inside information:** valuable information about future economic performance that is not generally available to the public

**insolvent:** a financial condition in which the value of one's assets is less than the value of one's liabilities

**insourcing:** the use of domestic workers to perform a service traditionally done by foreign workers

**institutions:** the basic rules, customs, and practices of society

**interest group:** a collection of individuals with common aims

**itemized deductions:** specific types of expenses (such as taxes levied by another jurisdiction) that lawfully may be deducted from income when computing taxable income

**labor force:** individuals aged 16 and over who either have jobs or are looking and available for work

**labor supply curve:** a schedule showing the quantity of labor supplied at each wage rate

**liabilities:** amounts owed; the legal claims against an individual or against an institution by those who are not owners of that institution

**long-run supply curve:** a schedule showing the amounts of goods and services that sellers are willing and able to produce and sell over the long term

**long-term liability:** a legally enforceable claim against one's assets extending beyond one year

**loophole:** a provision of the tax code that enables a narrow group of beneficiaries to achieve a lower effective tax rate

**Luddites:** followers of General Ned Ludd who, early in the nineteenth century, led destructive protests against mechanization in English textile mills; a term used today to refer to people who object to technological change

**lump-sum tax cut:** a reduction in taxes that is independent of income or other economic factors to which taxes are normally tied

**mandates:** in the context of governments, regulations or laws that require other governments, private individuals, or firms to spend money to achieve goals specified by the government

**marginal benefits:** the additional rewards from an activity

**marginal costs:** the additional sacrifice due to an activity

**marginal tax rate:** the percentage of the last dollar earned that is paid in taxes

**median age:** the age that separates the older half of the population from the younger half

**medium of exchange:** any asset that sellers will generally accept as payment

**mercantilists:** believers in the doctrine of mercantilism, which asserted (among other things) that exports were the principal objective of international trade, because they permitted the accumulation of gold

**merchandise deficit:** an excess of imports of goods over exports of goods

**monetary policy:** the use of changes in the amount of money in circulation to affect interest rates, credit markets, inflation (or deflation), and unemployment

**monetary rule:** a stipulation specifying that the central bank ensure that the money supply grows at a rate that is fixed and independent of current economic developments

**monetary standard:** a social agreement that a particular asset will serve as a medium of exchange, unit of accounting, and store of value

**money laundering:** engaging in transactions that make illegally earned profits appear to be the result of lawful ventures

**money supply:** the sum of checkable deposits and currency in the hands of the public

**mortgages:** debts that are incurred to buy a house and provide that if the debt is not paid, the house can be sold by the creditor and the proceeds used to pay that debt

**Multifiber Agreement (MFA):** international trade agreement established in 1974 that specified a system of *quotas* limiting imports of textiles and clothing

**natural resource endowments:** the collection of naturally occurring minerals (such as oil and iron ore) and living things (such as forests and fish stocks) that can be used to produce goods and services

**net public debt:** includes only that portion of the public debt that is owned outside of the government issuing it

**net worth:** the excess of assets over liabilities

**new economy:** a description given to the American economy to reflect its growing reliance on information technology

**nominal interest rate:** the premium, in percent per year, that people are willing to pay to have dollars sooner rather than later

**normal good:** a good for which the demand increases as people's income or wealth grows

**opportunity cost:** the highest-valued, next best alternative that must be sacrificed to obtain something

**optimal currency area:** a geographic or political area within which the advantages of having a single monetary unit or currency are at their greatest

**outsourcing:** the use of labor in another country to perform service work traditionally done by domestic workers

**pay-as-you-go system:** a scheme in which current cash outflows are funded (paid for) with current cash inflows

**payroll taxes:** taxes that are levied on income specifically generated by workforce participation and that are generally earmarked for spending on specific programs, such as Social Security

**per capita income:** gross domestic product (GDP), divided by population

**permanent income:** the sustained or average level of income that one expects will be observed over a long period of time

**personal exemptions:** tied to the number of persons in a household, the amount of income that lawfully may be excluded in computing taxable income due to the presence of these persons

**physical capital:** the productive capacity of physical assets, such as buildings

**positive externalities:** the excess of the social benefits of an action above the private benefits that accrue to the person responsible for that action

**price level:** the average current year cost, measured relative to the average base year cost, of a typical basket of goods and services

**production possibilities curve:** a curve representing all possible combinations of total output that could be produced, given the efficient use of a given amount of productive resources

**productivity:** output per unit of input

**profits:** the difference between revenue and cost

**property and contract rights:** legal rules governing the use and exchange of property and the enforceable agreements between people or businesses

**protectionism:** economic policy of promoting favored domestic industries through the use of high *tariffs* and *quotas* and other trade restrictions to reduce imports

**protectionist:** any attitude or policy that seeks to prevent foreigners from competing with domestic firms or individuals

**public debt:** the amount of money owed by a government to its creditors

**publicly traded corporations:** corporations whose stock can be purchased or sold on major public stock exchanges, such as the New York Stock Exchange

**purchasing power:** a measure of the amount of goods and services that can be purchased with a given amount of money

**quota:** limit on the amount of a good that may be imported; generally used to reduce imports so as to protect the economic interests of domestic industries that compete with the imports

**quota-hopping:** selecting the foreign location in which a good will be produced because the low-cost location is prevented by quotas from supplying the good

**random walk:** a pattern of price (or other) movements in which the best expectation of a future value is today's value, and in which the variability of price (or other entity) is constant over time

**rationing:** allocating scarce goods among competing claimants

**real federal discretionary spending:** inflation-adjusted spending by the federal government outside of so-called entitlement programs, such as Medicare

**real gross domestic product (real GDP):** the inflation-adjusted level of new, domestically produced, final goods and services

**real interest rate:** the premium, in percent per year, that people are willing to pay to have goods sooner rather than later

**real per capita GDP:** GDP corrected for inflation and divided by the population

**real purchasing power:** the amount of goods and services that can be acquired with an asset whose value is expressed in terms of the monetary unit of account (such as the dollar)

**real wages:** wages adjusted for changes in the price level

**recession:** a decline in the level of overall business activity

**regional free trade agreement:** an arrangement among several nations in a geographic region that reduces trade barriers among them

**relative prices:** prices of goods and services compared to the prices of other goods and services; costs of goods and services measured in terms of other commodities

**replacement cost:** what would have to be given up today to replace an asset

**repressed inflation:** inflation that occurs during price controls but does not show up in official price statistics

**reserve currency:** a currency held by private or government banks to enable them to meet the demands of depositors and to assure depositors of the ability of the bank to meet its obligations

**reserves:** assets held by depository institutions, typically in the form of currency held at the institution or as non-interest-bearing deposits held at the central bank

**resources:** any items capable of satisfying wants or suitable for transformation into goods capable of satisfying wants

**rule of law:** the principle that relations between individuals, businesses, and the government are governed by clearly enumerated rules that apply to everyone in society

**scarcity:** a state of the world in which there are limited resources but unlimited wants, implying that we must make choices among alternatives

**share of stock:** claim to a specified portion of future net cash flows (or profits) of a corporation

**shareholders:** owners of *shares of stock* in a corporation

**solvent:** a financial condition in which the value of one's assets is greater than the value of one's liabilities

**stockbroker:** a middleman who sells *shares of stock* to individuals

**store of value:** the ability to retain value over time

**subsidies:** government payments for the production of specific goods, generally intended to raise the profits of the firms producing those goods

**supply:** the willingness and ability to sell goods

**tariff:** tax levied only on imports; generally used to reduce imports so as to protect the economic interests of domestic industries that compete with the imports

**tax bracket:** a range of income over which a specific marginal tax rate applies

**tax rate:** the percentage of a dollar of income that must be paid in taxes

**tax rebate:** a return of some previously paid taxes

**trade barriers:** legal rules imposed by a nation that raise the costs of foreign firms seeking to sell goods in that nation; for example, *tariffs*

**trade deficit:** an excess of the value of imports of goods and services over the value of the exports of goods and services

**trade surplus:** an excess of the value of exports of goods and services over the value of the imports of goods and services

**transfer payments:** money payments made by governments for which no goods and services are received in return

**turnover:** the rate at which new employees replace old ones

**undocumented aliens:** new immigrants who have entered the country illegally and, thus, do not have the proper documents allowing them to legally remain as residents

**unemployment rate:** the number of persons looking and available for work, divided by the labor force

**unit of accounting:** a measure by which prices are expressed, that is, the common denominator of a price system

**wants:** the desires, aspirations, or preferences of individuals

**wealth:** the present value of all current and future income

**World Trade Organization (WTO):** an association of more than 145 nations around the world that helps reduce trade barriers among its members and handles international trade disputes among them

# Selected References and Web Links

## Chapter 1  Rich Nation, Poor Nation

Easterly, William, and Ross Levine. 2002. "Tropics, Germs, and Crops: How Endowments Influence Economic Development." *NBER Working Paper* no. w9106, National Bureau of Economic Research, Inc.

Mahoney, Paul G. "The Common Law and Economic Growth: Hayek Might Be Right." *Journal of Legal Studies,* 30, no. 2 (2001): 503–25.

Rosenberg, Nathan, and L. E. Birdzell, Jr. *How the West Grew Rich.* New York: Basic Books, 1987.

World Bank Group. http://www.worldbank.org

## Chapter 2  Return of the Luddites: Technophobia and Economic Growth

Evenson, R. E., and D. Gollin. "Assessing the Impact of the Green Revolution, 1960 to 2000." *Science* 300 (May 2, 2003): 758–62.

Lomborg, Bjorn. *The Skeptical Environmentalist: Measuring the Real State of the World.* Cambridge: Cambridge University Press, 2001.

Meiners, Roger E., and Andrew P. Morriss. "Property Rights and Pesticides." *PERC Policy Series* (Bozeman) 22, (2001).

Mokyr, Joel. *Lever of Riches: Technological Creativity and Economic Progress.* Oxford: Oxford University Press, 1990.

## Chapter 3  The Dragon and the Tigers: Economic Growth in Asia

Hilsenrath, Jon E., and Rebecca Buckman. "Factory Employment is Falling Worldwide." *Wall Street Journal,* October 20, 2003, sec. A-1.

Peerenboom, Randall. *China's Long March toward Rule of Law.* New York: Cambridge University Press, 2002.

Young, Alwyn. "Gold into Base Metals: Productivity Growth in the People's Republic of China during the Reform Period."

*Journal of Political Economy* III, no. 6 (December 2003): 1220–62.

## Chapter 4    Immigrants and Economic Growth

Borjas, George J. 1998. "Immigration and Welfare Magnets." *NBER Working Paper* no. w6813, National Bureau of Economic Research, Inc.

Borjas, George J. *Heaven's Door: Immigration Policy and the American Economy.* Princeton: Princeton University Press, 1999.

Borjas, George J. March 2002. "The Impact of Welfare Reform on Immigrant Welfare Use," Center for Immigration Studies.

## Chapter 5    Outsourcing and Economic Growth

Council of Economic Advisers. *Economic Report of the President.* Washington, DC: U.S. Government Printing Office, 2004.

Garten, Jeffrey E. "Offshoring: You Ain't Seen Nothin' Yet," *Business Week,* June 21, 2004, p. 28.

Gnuschke, John E., Jeff Wallace, Dennis R. Wilson, and Stephen C. Smith. 2004. "Outsourcing Production and Jobs: Costs and Benefits." *Business Perspectives* 16, no. 2 (Spring 2004): 12–18.

Irwin, Douglas A. "Free-Trade Worriers." *Wall Street Journal,* August 9, 2004, sec. A-12.

## Chapter 6    What's in a Word? Plenty, If It's the *R* Word

Business Cycle Dating Committee. "The NBER's Recession Dating Procedure." National Bureau of Economic Research, Inc. http://nber.org/cycles/recessions.html (October 21, 2003).

Conference Board. Business Cycle Indicators. http://www. globalindicators.org

Layton, Allan P., and Anirvan Banerji. "What is a Recession?: A Reprise." *Applied Economics* 35, no. 16 (November 10, 2003): 1789–97.

U.S. Department of Commerce. Bureau of Economic Analysis. http://www.bea.doc.gov

## Chapter 7    The Case of the Disappearing Workers

Benjamin, Daniel K., and Kent G.P. Matthews. *U.S. and U.K. Unemployment Between the Wars: A Doleful Story.* London: Institute for Economic Affairs, 1992.

Darby, Michael R. "Three-and-a-Half Million U.S. Employees Have Been Mislaid: Or, an Explanation of Unemployment, 1934–1941." *Journal of Political Economy* 84, no. 1 (February 1976): 1–16.

U.S. Department of Labor. Bureau of Labor Statistics. http://www.bls.gov

Wallis, John Joseph, and Daniel K. Benjamin. "Public Relief and Unemployment in the Great Depression." *Journal of Economic History* (March 1981): 97–102.

## Chapter 8    The Graying of the Workforce

Congressional Budget Office. "Baby Boomers' Retirement Prospects: An Overview." November 2003. http://www.cbo.gov/showdoc.cfm?index=4863&sequence=0

Lockwood, Nancy R. "The Aging Workforce: The Reality of the Impact of Older Workers and Eldercare in the Workplace," *HRMagazine,* July 2004, pp. S48–59.

McDonald, Peter, and Rebecca Kippen. "Labor Supply Prospects in 16 Developed Countries, 2000–2050." *Population and Development Review* 27, no. 1 (March 2001): 1–30.

Niggle, Christopher. "The Political Economy of Social Security Reform Proposals." *Journal of Economic Issues* 34, no. 4 (December 2000): 789–805.

U.S. Department of Labor. Bureau of Labor Statistics. http://www.bls.gov

## Chapter 9    The Problem with Deflation

Bordo, Michael D., Michael J. Dueker, and David C. Wheelock. "Aggregate Price Shocks and Financial Instability: A Historical Analysis." *Economic Inquiry* 40, no. 4 (October 2002): 521–38.

Delong, J. Bradford, Ben S. Bernanke, and William B. English. "America's Historical Experience with Low Inflation." *Journal of Money, Credit & Banking* 32, no. 4 (November 2000): 979–1001.

Parker, Randall E., and Philip Rothman. "An Examination of the Asymmetric Effects of Money Supply Shocks in the Pre-World War I and Interwar Periods." *Economic Inquiry* 42, no. 1 (January 2004): 88–100.

Reifschneider, David, John C. Williams, Christopher A. Sims, and John B. Taylor. "Three Lessons for Monetary Policy in a Low-Inflation Era." *Journal of Money, Credit and Banking* 32, no. 4 (November 2000): 936–54.

## Chapter 10   The Problem with Inflation

Alchian, Armen A. and Reuben Kessel. "The Effects of Inflation." *Journal of Political Economy* 70, no. 6 (December 1962): 521–37.

Cagan, Phillip. "Monetary Dynamics of Hyperinflation." In *Studies in the Quantity Theory of Money,* edited by Milton Friedman. Chicago: University of Chicago Press, 1956.

Keynes, John Maynard. *The Economic Consequences of the Peace.* New York: Harcourt, Brace, and Howe, 1920.

## Chapter 11   The Futility of Price Controls

Alchian, Armen A. "Review of the Council of Economic Advisers Annual Report, 1972." *Journal of Money. Credit and Banking* 4, no. 4 (August 1972): 704–12.

Bernholz, Peter. *Monetary Regimes and Inflation: History, Economic and Political Relationships,* Cheltenham, UK: Edward Elgar, 2003.

Block, Walter, and Edgar Olsen (eds.). *Rent Control Myths and Realities: International Evidence of the Effects of Rent Control in Six Countries.* Vancouver: Fraser Institute, 1981.

## Chapter 12   The Return of Big Government

Birnbaum, Jeffrey H. "The Return of Big Government: Federal Spending is Skyrocketing, but Shockingly Little of It Is Related to Sept. 11," *Fortune,* September 16, 2002, p. 112.

"Can't Last: George Bush's Big-Government Conservatism," *The Economist* (US), January 10, 2004, p. 23.

Peterson, Peter G. "Hear No Deficit, See No Deficit, Speak No Deficit," *Fortune,* August 23, 2004, p. 48.

Pierce, Vanessa. "Wasteful Spending Thwarts Recovery," *Insight on the News,* August 19, 2003, p. 28.

U.S. Office of Management and Budget. Budget of the United States, Fiscal Year 2005. http://www.whitehouse.gov/omb/budget/

## Chapter 13    The Myths of Social Security

Congressional Budget Office. "Social Security: A Primer." September 2001. http://www.cbo.gov/showdoc.cfm?index=3213&sequence=0

Engelhardt, Gary V., and Jonathan Gruber. 2004. "Social Security and the Evolution of Elderly Poverty." *NBER Working Paper* No. w10466, National Bureau of Economic Research, Inc.

Oshio, Takashi. 2004. "Social Security and Trust Fund Management." *NBER Working Paper* no. w10444, National Bureau of Economic Research, Inc.

U.S. Social Security Administration. Social Security Online. http://www.ssa.gov

## Chapter 14    Tax Cuts: When They Matter, When They Don't

Congressional Budget Office. "Economic Stimulus: Evaluating Proposed Changes in Tax Policy." January 2002. http://www.cbo.gov/showdoc.cfm?index=3251&sequence=0

Feenberg, Daniel R., and James M. Poterba. "The Alternative Minimum Tax and Effective Marginal Tax Rates." *National Tax Journal* 57, no. 2 (June 2004): 407-27.

GPO Access. Budget of the United States Government: Main Page. http://www.access.gpo.gov/usbudget

Seater, John J. "Ricardian Equivalence." *Journal of Economic Literature* 31, no. 1 (March 1993): 142-90.

## Chapter 15    Simplifying the Federal Tax System (Don't Hold Your Breath)

Averett, Susan L., Edward N. Gamber, and Sheila Handy. "William E. Simon's Contribution to Tax Policy." *Atlantic Economic Journal* 31, no. 3 (September 2003): 233-41.

Willens, Robert, and Andrea J. Phillips. "Who Said the World Isn't Flat?" *Journal of Accountancy* 180, no. 5 (November 1995): 39–42.

## Chapter 16    Raising the Debt Ceiling—What's a Few Trillion Dollars, More or Less?

Chaddock, Gail Russell. "Congress Tiptoes Around Raising Debt Ceiling: Rules of Fiscal Restraint May Be Revised as Hill Looks to Increase Election-Year Budget." *Christian Science Monitor,* April 8, 2002, p. 02.

Congressional Budget Office. "Federal Debt and the Commitments of Federal Trust Funds." May 2003. http://www.cbo.gov/showdoc.cfm?index=3948&sequence=0

Neikirk, William. "U.S. Treasury to Tap Retirement Fund to Avoid Default." *Knight Ridder/Tribune News Service,* April 2, 2002, sec. K0376.

## Chapter 17    Bad Accounting by Uncle Sam

Kitchen, John. "Observed Relationships Between Economic and Technical Receipts Revisions in Federal Budget Projections." *National Tax Journal* 56, no. 2 (June 2003): 337–53.

Sloan, Allen. "Enron and Fuzzy Math: As the Accounting Scandal Unfolds, the U.S. Budget Surplus Vanishes," *Newsweek,* Feb 4, 2002, p. 22.

Congressional Budget Office. http://www.cbo.gov

## Chapter 18    The Future of the Fed:  New Economy versus Inflation Targeting

Gavin, William T. "Inflation Targeting: Why it Works and How to Make it Work Better," *Business Economics,* April 2004, p. 30–7.

Hayford Marc D., and A. G. Malliaris. "Monetary Policy and the U.S. Stock Market," *Economic Inquiry,* July 2004, pp. 387–401.

Schwartz, Anna J. "Asset Price Inflation and Monetary Policy." *Atlantic Economic Journal* 31, no. 1 (March 2003): 1–14.

## Chapter 19    Monetary Policy and Interest Rates

Demiralp, Selva, and Oscar Jorda. "The Response of Term Rates to Fed Announcements." *Journal of Money, Credit and Banking.* 36, no. 3 (June 2004): 387–405.

Preiss, Michael. "Fighting the Federal Reserve is a Losing Proposition." *Knight Ridder/Tribune Business News,* August 13, 2004, sec. ITEM04226170.

## Chapter 20    Beating the Market

Chari, V. V., and Patrick J. Kehoe. "Hot Money." *Journal of Political Economy,* III, no. 6 (December 2003): 1262–92.

Feinstone, Lauren J. "Minute by Minute: Efficiency, Normality and Randomness in Intra-Daily Asset Prices." *Journal of Applied Econometrics* 2, no. 1 (1987): 193–214.

Malkiel, Burton G. *A Random Walk Down Wall Street: Including a Life-Cycle Guide to Personal Investing.* New York: W.W. Norton, 1996.

Scheinkman, Jose A., and Wei Xiong. "Overconfidence and Speculative Bubbles." *Journal of Political Economy* III, no. 6 (December 2003): 1183–1219.

## Chapter 21    The Case against Cash

Benjamin, Daniel K., and Roger LeRoy Miller. *Undoing Drugs: Beyond Legalization.* New York: Basic Books, 1991.

Kochan, Nick. "Money-Laundering Controls Look All Washed Up." *Euromoney* 34, no. 413 (September 2003): 94–7.

## Chapter 22    Don't Worry: Your Deposits Are Insured

Allen, Franklin, and Douglas Gale. "Competition and Financial Stability." *Journal of Money, Credit and Banking.* 36, no. 3 (June 2004): S453–80.

Bordo, M., H. Rockoff, and A. Redish. "The U.S. Banking System from a Northern Exposure: Stability versus Efficiency." *Journal of Economic History* 54(1994): 325–41.

Diamond, D., and P. Dybvig. "Bank Runs, Deposit Insurance, and Liquidity." *Journal of Political Economy* 91(1983): 401–19.

Friedman, Milton, and Anna J. Schwartz. *A Monetary History of the United States, 1867–1960.* Princeton: Princeton University Press, 1963.

## Chapter 23    The Opposition to Free Trade

Frankel, J. A., and D. Romer. "Does Trade Cause Growth?" *American Economic Review* 89 (1999): 379–99.

Makki, Shiva S., and Agapi Somwaru. "Impact of Foreign Direct Investment and Trade on Economic Growth: Evidence from Developing Countries." *American Journal of Agricultural Economics* 86, no. 3 (August 2004): 795–801.

## Chapter 24  The $750,000 Job

Congressional Budget Office. "The Pros and Cons of Pursuing Free-Trade Agreements." July 2003. http://www.cbo.gov/showdoc.cfm?index=4458&sequence=0

Greider, William. "A New Giant Sucking Sound: China Is Taking Away Mexico's Jobs, as Globalization Enters a Fateful New Stage," *The Nation,* December 31, 2001, p. 22.

"Stolen Jobs? Offshoring," *The Economist* (US), December 13, 2003, p. 15.

## Chapter 25  The Trade Revolution in Textiles

Congressional Budget Office. "The Domestic Costs of Sanctions on Foreign Commerce." March 1999. http://www.cbo.gov/showdoc.cfm?index=1133&sequence=0&from=1

De Jonquieres, Guy. "Clothes on the Line." *Financial Times,* July 19, 2004, p. 13. (This was the first in a week-long series in the *Financial Times,* entitled "The Textile Revolution.")

Magnusson, Paul. "Where Free Trade Hurts," *Business Week,* December 15, 2003, p. 22.

## Chapter 26  The Trade Deficit

Congressional Budget Office. "Causes and Consequences of the Trade Deficit: An Overview." March 2000. http://www.cbo.gov/showdoc.cfm?index=1897&sequence=0

Congressional Budget Office. "The Decline in the U.S. Current-Account Balance Since 1991." August 2004. http://www.cbo.gov/showdoc.cfm?index=5722&sequence=0

Cooper, James C., and Kathleen Madigan. "The Trade Deficit May Soon Cause Less Pain: A Worker Dollar and Stronger Global Demand Will Slow Down the Beast," *Business Week,* July 26, 2004, p. 27.

## Chapter 27    The Dollar Standard

Couchene, T. J., and Youssef, G. M. "The Demand for International Reserves." *Journal of Political Economy* 75, no. 3 (June 1967): 404–13.

Frenkel, Jacob A. "The Demand for International Reserves by Developed and Less-Developed Countries." *Economica* 41, no. 1 (1974): 14–24.

Mundell., Robert A. "What the Euro Means for the Dollar and the International Monetary System." *Atlantic Economic Journal* 26, no. 3 (September 1998): 227–37.

## Chapter 28    The Euro: Promise and Peril

Cabos, Karen, and Nikolaus A. Siegfried. "Controlling Inflation in Euroland." *Applied Economics* 36, no. 6 (April 10, 2004): 549–58.

European Central Bank. http://www.ecb.int

Mundell., Robert A. "The Significance of the Euro in the International Monetary System," *American Economist* 47, no. 2 (Fall 2003): 27–39.

# Index